Win-Win Negotiations for Couples

Win Win
Negotiations for Couples

Para Research
Gloucester
Massachusetts

Win-Win Negotiations for Couples
by Charlotte Whitney

Library of Congress Card Number: 85-072095
International Standard Book Number: 0-914918-66-4

Edited by Camilla Ayers and Emily McKeigue
Typeset in 10 pt. Paladium on Compugraphic MCS/8400
Typeset by Camilla Ayers
Printed by Alpine Press, Inc. on 55-pound SRT II Paper
Cover design by Bob Boeberitz
Cover illustration by Tom Speck
208 pages

Published by Para Research, Inc.
85 Eastern Avenue
Gloucester, Massachusetts 01930

Manufactured in the United States of America

First Printing, January 1986, 5,000 copies

Contents

Preface

Early in my career I became exposed to the "win-win" concept while working with management development seminars at the University of Michigan Graduate School of Business Administration. While the concept was being applied specifically in the workplace, I saw clear implications for interpersonal relationships, particularly primary relationships. All too frequently couples engage in arguments until a win-lose position is established. The result is anger, resentment, and guilt. If, instead, a win-win approach were applied, then there would be potential for growth, nurturing, and heightened love.

Later, working in the field of communication and counseling, I found many couples who desperately wanted to establish a good primary relationship but were lacking the necessary communication skills. They would assume that their partners understood their needs without communicating those needs to each other. Frequently their needs were not in conflict, but the couple would be too embroiled in hostility to recognize the situation. By establishing an adversarial position early in the communication process, the couple would fail to communicate essential details of their needs. The purpose of this book is to aid couples in communicating those details in an environment where both partners emerge as "winners."

In order to obtain background material for the book, I interviewed approximately forty couples over the course of two years. The interviews covered the couples' decision-making processes in several areas including careers, finances, vacations, household chores and other particularly problematic areas. Whenever possible I interviewed the couples together; however, in some instances because of time or work constraints I interviewed them separately. In a few instances I interviewed only one partner in the relationship. All of the couples were heterosexual, either married or living together. While I made no attempt to have a statistically random sample, I did follow a standard structured interview. Several recurrent themes emerged. They provided structure and direction for the book.

The first chapter defines the win-win approach to negotiations along with the related topics of personal risk taking, trust, and the logical and emotional components of joint decision making. I also have included several tools for decision making, borrowed from management science. The details of setting up a personal negotiation session along with rules of conduct are also described in this chapter.

The rest of the book is organized around subjects which are sources of conflict for many couples. They include issues dealing with lifestyle, personal finances, career, children, household chores, sex, vacations, holidays, leisure, housewives and househusbands, and two-paycheck couples.

As more and more couples move toward egalitarian relationships, the negotiation process will become critical in resolving differences. The tools in this book should provide a starting point for couples working toward stronger, happier relationships. Through professional observation and personal experience, I have come to believe that win-win decisions are the most satisfying, and a cooperative approach to life the most fulfilling. I sincerely hope that after reading this book you will share this belief. More important, however, I hope that using these tools will enable you to establish a better, more intimate relationship.

Charlotte Whitney
Ann Arbor, Michigan

Acknowledgments

I am indebted to the numerous couples who openly and candidly shared with me their personal successes and failures. Their stories have provided me with much material for this book. I would like to thank Scott Kunst, who has made many useful suggestions, and my editor, Emily McKeigue, who provided professional direction and positive reinforcement. My typist Joyce Wodka, my colleague Janet LaRose, and my daycare provider Fran Proctor have provided extraordinary professional and personal support. Finally, I could not write so positively about win-win negotiations if I had not personally benefited from the process. I owe much to my husband, Dr. William J. Thomson. Bill and I have negotiated countless issues from buying groceries to having babies. This book is dedicated to him.

1

Learning to Negotiate as Winners

Negotiation. For many of us the word has negative connotations. It brings to mind haggling over the price of a used car, protracted battles between labor and management, and embittered court settlements. Chances are if you've been involved in this kind of negotiation, you found the experience unpleasant and exhausting—not something you'd like to try at home with your partner.

Why do we hold such negative views about negotiation? Because we have always perceived the negotiation process as *adversarial*. There's a winner and a loser, and in order to establish a one-up position it's not uncommon to downgrade, belittle, or insult the opposing side. It's an artificial situation where you dare not disclose your true thoughts or feelings for fear your opponents will use the information against you.

"Win-win" negotiating takes a different approach. Instead of opposing each other, both parties work together to find mutual—often creative— solutions to problems at hand. Using the win-win approach both parties attempt to meet each other's needs. Both parties see that there is a long-range payoff for maintaining good relations with one another. Today's mutual gain may be multiplied tomorrow. And tomorrow you're going to be much more interested in working with someone who has been considerate of your needs.

Couples have much to gain by adopting a win-win approach to problem-solving. If, for instance, two hours after dinner the dishes haven't been cleaned up, a couple has several choices. One is not to clean them up. However, if they both agree the table needs to be cleared and the dishes washed, then they face several additional options. They could fight about it until one person gives in and decides to clean up. This would resolve the issue, but both individuals likely would carry some residual bad feelings that would influence future interactions with each other. Chances are the loser (the dishwasher) would feel some anger and resentment, and the winner some guilt. This could result in another fight the following evening if the same pattern is followed. Even if there's not another fight, the residual feelings could cause problems about some other issue.

If, instead, the couple had taken a win-win approach, several different outcomes would have been possible:

1. One person could have agreed to clear the table and the other to wash the dishes.
2. One person could have agreed to do all the clean-up in return for an I.O.U. from the other person for a later date.
3. They could have divided the work fifty-fifty, sharing both the table clearing and dishwashing.
4. One person could have agreed to do all the clean-up. In return, the other person would be responsible for a different chore, perhaps some laundry or vacuuming.

Obviously none of these options is right or wrong. They are simply examples of solutions in which both people end up feeling good—not only about completing the chores, but more important, about each other.

Put simply, win-win negotiations are those in which both parties end up as "winners." Each person may compromise a bit, and perhaps trade off an item here or there, but in the end the goal is accomplished and both people feel positive about one another.

Win-Win Examples

How are win-win negotiations different from other methods of decision making? Is there a step-by-step process? How can you apply it to real life situations? Let's look at three examples to see how real people work out win-win solutions.

Jogging vs. Dinner

Natalie and Vince were at loggerheads about his arriving home late from work each evening after stopping at the track to jog five miles. Vince was aware of Natalie's mounting anger but was unwilling to give up his jogging, which he viewed as an emotional outlet and essential to his health. Natalie proposed a negotiation session to discuss the problem and work out a solution. They scheduled it for an evening they both had free.

Natalie came to the session with a list of her concerns:

1. She resented the fact that she always had to make dinner since she was always the first one home.
2. She resented the fact that she frequently had dinner ready an hour before Vince arrived; often she was hungry and the wait seemed interminable.
3. She couldn't really enjoy dinner with Vince when she was so angry with him for being late.

Vince's concern was simple: he needed four jogging work-outs a week. Going jogging after work was best because it let him wind down from work. Also, it didn't cut into the weekend.

An important discovery early in the discussion was that Vince indicated that he didn't expect Natalie to prepare dinner every evening—or at all, for that matter. He figured she always cooked because she enjoyed it.

After more talk, they came up with the following options.

1. Vince could jog early in the morning before work. This would mean they would not be able to have coffee and read the paper together—an activity they both enjoyed.
2. Vince could jog twice a week after work and twice on weekends. On the weeknights he wasn't jogging Natalie and Vince would trade off cooking dinner. On the nights he did jog, they would have leftovers or pizza or go out.
3. Natalie could take up jogging and join Vince at the track after work. Afterwards they would fix dinner together.
4. Vince could continue his regular jogging schedule, but they wouldn't have dinner together. He would make a sandwich when he got home or have whatever was on hand. Natalie could make her own dinner arrangements as she pleased.

Each option was discussed at length. They decided options one and three weren't likely to be successful. Vince just wasn't a morning person and probably wouldn't get up early enough to jog. Neither did Natalie feel comfortable with the idea of taking up jogging. She had tried it a couple of times already and didn't like it. Option number four had more appeal, but its largest disadvantage was that it severed the companionship between them during the evening.

They finally decided to try option number two for a four-week trial period. They established Mondays and Wednesdays as dinner nights and Tuesdays and Thursdays as jogging nights. They also set a date to talk about this arrangement after the four weeks were up. Both Vince and Natalie were pleased with the outcome of the discussion. Vince was able to maintain a jogging schedule and Natalie was able to clear up some misconceptions about fixing dinner. Both were pleased with the care that they displayed for each other. Clearly they valued their companionship and their relationship highly. Their goal was win-win.

Negotiating Vacation Plans

Joan and Dave had each arranged with their employers for a three-week vacation. Joan, who had never been to Europe, had been fantasizing a "dream trip" through eight countries. She had talked to travel agents and figured out a trip that was within their financial means. Dave, who travels extensively on his job, had been to Europe on vacation three times before he met Joan. His idea of a good vacation was to stay home, take it easy, and do a little gardening.

When Joan and Dave started discussing vacation plans they both readily recognized how far apart they stood. Both understood why the other preferred a particular type of vacation, but that did not change their own feelings. They started by discussing the choices that were obvious: either they would both go to Europe or both stay home. However, as the discussion continued, they both began to mention other, more creative options open to them. They came up with the following list:

1. Joan could go to Europe by herself or with her friend Donna, and Dave could stay home.
2. They both would stay home this summer, and both go to Europe next year.
3. They both could go to Europe, but spend at least one week at a quiet Mediterranean resort instead of traveling so extensively.
4. Joan could go on the entire three-week "dream trip" and Dave would spend half of the vacation time at home and join her for half of the European tour.

By the end of their discussion, they both were feeling positive about the third and fourth options. They were also feeling very good about their willingness to look at each other's situation and empathize with the other person. Both were genuinely concerned about meeting the other's needs, as well as their own. They ultimately decided on the third option, which worked out well. Both Joan and Dave felt much better than if one or the other had simply decided to go to Europe or stay home. There was no resentment from the one who "lost" or guilt from the one who "won." Their decision was clearly "win-win."

Naming the Baby

Veronica and Frank had no difficulty with the big decision: they both wanted a baby. But another issue was giving them a lot of trouble: what to name the baby. A year ago they had been through a series of arguments over naming their new kitten, which was surprising since they rarely fought over such little issues. In that situation, Veronica had given in and the kitten was named "Johnson," Frank's choice. Since that time Veronica had felt that Johnson was more Frank's cat than hers. The whole naming process had left real scars.

For a few months the couple avoided discussing names for the baby, but as the delivery date approached, Frank brought up the topic again. Veronica decided that this time she would not give in but stand firm on her choice of names. Frank, sensing Veronica's anger, suggested a different approach. He purchased a book listing names and suggested to Veronica that she go through them and select her top twenty-five choices for boys and girls. Frank did the same.

Later the couple sat down together and compared their lists. Three girls' names and seven boys' names appeared on both of their lists. They discussed each of these potential names, coming quickly to a decision on their top choice for a girl. The discussion of boys' names didn't lead to any decision so they decided to put it on hold for a few days.

Before they started discussing the boys' names again, Veronica suggested that they individually rank each of the seven boys' names in order of preference. After doing this they compared rankings and found that two names emerged near the top of both lists. They used these names as a starting point for their discussion, and ended up with one of these names as their top choice for a first name and Veronica's family name as a boy's middle name. After they made the decision, the couple went out to dinner to celebrate. They were feeling extremely pleased with their choices, and they even had names to use for a second child. Unlike naming the kitten, this was a win-win decision.

Negotiating Little Deals

In many situations negotiating win-win solutions to problems is as simple as "let's make a deal." It will take only a moment or two to work something out. "I'll go buy the groceries now, but would you put them away when I get home?" or "I'll drive to the family reunion and back if you'll make a dish for the potluck," or "I don't mind buying the turntable if you'll buy the speakers." Most of us make these deals with frequency on a daily basis.

Sometimes they become a little more involved, like this:

"I really want to take a nap this afternoon. Why don't you wait and buy the groceries tomorrow?"

"No, I want to work in the yard tomorrow. How about if I buy the groceries today and put them away, if you fix the blue chair sometime this week?"

"Okay."

When negotiating little deals, compromises, trade-offs, and I.O.U.'s are essential. Perhaps you both dislike shoveling snow, so you compromise and do it together or alternate from snowfall to snowfall. Or you find that changes at work make it impossible for you to pick up your son from the daycare center. You suggest to your partner that you'll shovel the snow as a trade-off for picking up your son. I.O.U.'s work the same way. For example, you are facing final exams and it's your turn to clean the house and do the laundry. You ask your partner to do it for you. You then owe your partner an extra house-cleaning and laundry job.

As you begin to use compromise, trade-offs, and I.O.U.'s, you will find that it becomes easier and easier. You will find mutually satisfying solutions in a rather relaxed, informal manner.

While most "little deals" are easy to negotiate, it isn't always the case. Frequently couples fall into behavioral patterns that are difficult to break, particularly due to sex-role conditioning. Traditionally women have not been expected to repair cars, nor have men been expected to change diapers. Women have not been expected to fix faucets, nor men to make curtains. You know the stereotypes. Of course, all of this is slowly changing, but the patterns remain with us, often unconsciously. So for many couples, chores like washing dishes, buying groceries, and fixing cars are not negotiated. They're just part of the routine, depending on the established patterns.

People also bring expectations from their families. "Dad always read bedtime stories so you should, too." "Mom always cleaned the fish after we went fishing." "We always had to wait until after Christmas breakfast to look in our stockings." "That's the way it's going to be. Negotiations closed." Breaking established patterns is difficult.

There are many other situations in which little deals just won't work. He gets transferred and she doesn't want to move. She wants another child and he doesn't. He wants to buy a yacht and she doesn't. In these situations, full-blown formalized negotiations are in order. You will need to arrange a time and place to sit down and look at the problem in depth in order to explore the troublesome areas and look for solutions that meet the needs of both people. Then, looking at all the options, the couple will decide on the one that best fits both of their needs.

Formalized Negotiations:
Big Deals and Troublesome Little Deals

When you are not able to come to a quick decision with compromises, trade-offs, and I.O.U.'s, something else is needed. This is the time for a formalized negotiation session. This means scheduling some time together to work out a mutually satisfactory solution to an unresolved problem—large or small. "Big deal" issues might include deciding whether to adopt a child, accept a new job offer, or invest your savings in a speculative business venture.

Also, couples frequently need more formalized sessions to work out the irritating problems in their relationship. These troublesome "little deals" might include splitting up household chores and deciding who stays home with the children when they are sick.

Working out solutions to "small" problems, in fact, may be useful in developing your negotiation skills. Once you begin to feel comfortable with negotiations as a concept and the win-win approach in general, you will be able to apply the concepts much more readily. If you reach agreement about who sets the mousetraps and who gets rid of the dead mice, you may feel more confident about tackling the question of adopting a child or accepting a job offer.

When setting up a formalized negotiation session with your partner, it is important to convey your conviction. Make clear your desire to work out a solution that is mutually satisfactory. You should be straightforward, calm, and nonjudgmental. If the topic has been a source of conflict in the past, let your partner know that your intent is not to reopen wounds, but to work out the problem.

Be clear in stating your plans for the negotiation session. If you are going to bring some proposed solutions to the meeting, invite your partner to do that, too. If any kind of advanced research is needed before the session, allow your partner the opportunity to participate. If any reading (including this book) would enhance the session, invite your partner to share this material. It is extremely important that both of you see your involvement as equal.

If your partner is resistant to the idea of setting up a negotiation session, meet the resistance head on. If he states he can't meet in the morning, then schedule the meeting for the afternoon or evening. If she says that she thinks the current financial arrangement is just fine, then clearly and calmly explain that you are dissatisfied with it, and that your discontent is beginning to adversely affect your relationship.

Making Win-Win Work for You

Commitment from Both Partners

In order for the win-win concept to work, both partners must be committed to it. Both people must recognize that there's more to gain from solving a problem in a new way that enhances their relationship, than scoring I-win, you-lose victories. Win-win solutions are particularly difficult in a relationship where there's already a lot of anger, autocratism, and lack of communication. It's easy to lose your focus by getting caught up in proving a point or displaying an emotion. Flaunting that "I'm right" and "you're wrong" may provide some satisfaction in the short run, but it sabotages the real goal of building and strengthening your relationship.

Both partners must be committed to win-win, and both must be willing to forgo some victories and losses. In everyday terms this means doing a few things that you may think unnecessary, but that are critical to your partner's sense of self. For instance, my husband Bill insists on his privacy, and I always knock on the door before entering any room he's in—even if it is my own study! Similarly Bill never drives my car without asking. For us these are essential courtesies—which might be just a nuisance for other couples.

It's important not to sabotage the negotiations. A frequent problem with couples starting the negotiation process is that one partner will covertly set up a situation he or she knows has a high probability of failure for the other person. Then if the partner doesn't meet his end of the agreement, she can state, "I knew you'd never do it." Or he can say, "If you really loved me, you would have gotten it done regardless." There's also the martyr version which goes like this, "Oh, all right, I knew you'd never be able to do it anyway, so I'll continue to do it at a great cost to my own personal happiness."

If you recognize a factor that will make it difficult for either you or your partner to carry through with an obligation, it's important to bring this up rather than set yourself up for failure. For example, you might say, "How will you be able to fix dinner on Tuesday night? That's when you play racquetball after work. How about Wednesday night instead?" It comes back to the fact that in order to have a win-win situation, you both need to *want* to win, and you both need to set up situations where you *can* win.

The Necessity for Trust

Win-win negotiations are also dependent on trust. You must trust your partner in several ways. First, you must trust one another to be honest. Unless you are both open and honest the negotiations are likely to fail. This means giving an accurate account of how you perceive a situation and your relationship. It also means stating this in a constructive manner. Honesty is not an excuse for being rude or insulting. If you think your partner should lose some weight, simply state, "I'd like you to lose some weight," without reference to cows, pigs, hippos, or other corpulent beasts.

On another level you must be able to trust your partner's willingness to follow through on an agreement. Give your partner the opportunity to keep the agreement. Trust your partner as an adult to live up to his or her end of the bargain. Anything less is putting yourself in a parent-child situation.

On still another level you need to trust one another for support if there is difficulty in carrying out the agreement. If she has agreed to paint the living room on Saturday, but later gets called in to work for the day, then you need to help her make arrangements for painting on another day. It's important to problem solve together and find the next best option if you run into a snag.

Risk-Taking

Risk-taking is a large part of the change process. When you make changes you expose your vulnerability to those around you. You may have to face rejection if you decide to change jobs; you may have to face less than straight A's if you choose to go back to school after twenty years. You will have to take some risks if you buy a house or other property. But if you calculate your decision with the best information available, you are better off taking some risks than remaining stagnant.

When facing such risks, it is often helpful to seek out resources. Some of the best resources are people who have already faced the situation you are about to face. Look for information from those who have taken similar risks and succeeded. They may be able to suggest informative books, articles and professional people to help you with your decision.

Fear of failure keeps too many people from making changes and improving their lifestyles. Also the lack of 100 percent certainty becomes a "logical" excuse for many people not to take risks. If this is your situation, you may want to consider the best case and worst case scenarios associated with each decision. You may find that the worst case can be endured and is well worth the risk. Another useful technique is to ease into a new situation gradually. Take one course instead of enrolling in a full load of classes. Start moonlighting in your new career choice rather than immediately quitting your job.

Establishing Cooperation as a Lifestyle and Success as a Worldview

Cooperation as a Lifestyle

At the heart of win-win negotiations is the idea that a cooperative approach is best. If you view your partner as your opponent, the odds for a successful problem-solving session are greatly diminished. Cooperation is a much better approach, not only to decision making, but to life in general.

Let me give you a personal example. When I started working at the business school placing students on internships, there was a lot of rivalry between the liberal arts college and my area. In fact, as far as I could see the two units did not communicate, even though we both were doing essentially the same thing, placing students on jobs in the business community. After a maternity leave and a promotion, I came back as director of the program at the same time the liberal arts program had appointed a new director. She was a person who had a teaching background and values similar to mine. We tested the waters slowly, shared information, and were both surprised to find out what valuable sources of information we could be for one another. The end result has been that by cooperating closely and sharing information and personal contacts, we both have benefited by increased productivity and more professional programs.

This cooperative attitude and approach carries over into many other facets of life as well. In the above example it was easy to measure the outcome of our cooperation. We ended up with a certain number of student job placements that would not have been achieved otherwise. Unfortunately, the results are not so easily measured in most situations.

Nevertheless, I wouldn't doubt that you will have more positive outcomes if you take a cooperative rather than adversarial approach with the following groups of people: teachers, health professionals, retail clerks, secretaries, supervisors, restaurant personnel, childcare workers, librarians, airline personnel, social workers, engineers, gas station attendants, and just about everybody else. It's as simple as this: If you cooperate with other people in a positive fashion, they almost always will reciprocate. And yes, that includes your partner.

Success as a Worldview

Frequently individuals who have achieved success in various facets of life are considered "lucky." If you look closely at those individuals, though, almost always you will find people who had a goal and were determined to work hard to achieve it, often at some personal sacrifice. Success rarely comes easily. Most people seek it out. The truly successful people I have met all have been positive thinkers; they have been realistic in their optimism, also. They plan carefully, get full information before making a decision, and work extremely hard at fulfilling their goals.

But what does all this have to do with win-win relationships? It comes down to the fact that how you view yourself and your success (or lack of success) will affect your relationship tremendously. If you are goal-oriented and enter a situation expecting a positive outcome, your odds for success are increased—at work or with your partner. If you expect success you will find creative solutions to achieve it, anywhere.

For instance, Paul was offered an opportunity by his company to take on an extra project. It was an assignment, however, that required him to travel out of state eight to twelve days a month. When discussing this with his wife Nancy, Paul was straightforward and realistic about the ramifications of this assignment on Nancy and his homelife. He did allow his enthusiasm to show by stating that the project would give him the experience needed to be transferred to the company's Denver location—a goal shared by both Paul and Nancy. The result of their discussion was that they jointly agreed that Paul should accept the assignment, recognizing that it would not be easy for Nancy on the days Paul would be out of town. She would have total responsibility of managing the household and their two-year-old daughter. However, they both agreed it would be worth it in the end if it meant that a move to Denver was a realistic outcome.

How Paul and Nancy handled the decision affected their attitudes over the next few months. Because Nancy viewed the decision as a joint one, she enthusiastically took on the extra responsibilities. Had Paul approached her in a different manner, stating that he had already made the decision and that she would have to suffer the consequences, it's likely that both he and Nancy would have had many more problems over the ensuing months. As it turned out, Paul's assignment resulted in a transfer to the Denver office the following year. They were both pleased that they had put up with Paul's schedule for a few months in order to attain a higher goal.

Think Positively But Be Realistic

While a positive attitude is important, that is not to say that blind optimism is a cure-all. There are too many dead-end jobs, bad business investments, and defective products to always "look at the bright side." There are also many people with personality problems too severe to consider them good risks for primary relationships. Sometimes getting out is the best route. Starting over may be difficult, in whatever area—career, education, or relationship. But in the long run it may be better than staying in a losing situation. If you feel like you're in over your head, it would be wise to seek professional help. Get the advice of experts and use some common sense in figuring out what's best for you. The "Using Counselors" section at the end of this chapter provides information on utilizing marriage counselors and therapists.

Bottom Lines

Certain issues in any relationship are not negotiable. These will vary from couple to couple, and will be linked to each individual's ethics, moral standards, or religion. Such issues are bottom-line standards; if you are at loggerheads with your partner about them you may well want to question staying in the relationship. Bottom line issues might include not having affairs, not using illicit drugs, not lying to one another, and not making major purchases without consulting each other. These are important issues of fundamental values and are not to be taken lightly.

Sometimes, however, people confuse their bottom line standards with other issues. For instance, John says he wants to have children and Rebecca says she doesn't. On the surface this issue is not negotiable. Unlike puppies, children cannot be bought and sold, tried out for a while and given away if they prove impossible. Children are a major life commitment. If one partner says no to having children and later "gives in," he or she is likely to be resentful of both the child and the partner.

However, if John and Rebecca's situation is such that Rebecca would like to have children, but is unwilling to interrupt her career for several years to stay home and raise them—then they have their issues confused. If the career issue is truly Rebecca's only objection to having children, then she and John have many options to consider. They include:

1. using childcare services such as daycare homes and daycare centers;
2. using relatives or neighbors for childcare;
3. working part-time (an option for both John and Rebecca);
4. John staying home to raise the kids.

There may be even more possibilities for John and Rebecca. They need to discuss their concerns completely and determine if they are dealing with a bottom line or not.

In another situation, Jackie has told her partner of six months, Jeff, that she refuses to live with anyone who smokes. Jeff recently started smoking again after quitting for a year. He says he doesn't want to quit right now, but he will in a few months or so. In this situation Jeff would certainly need to know Jackie's objection to his smoking. Is it a concern over his health?

Or her health? Is it because he smells like smoke? Or the house smells like smoke? Is it because he is setting a poor example for Jackie's children? If Jackie's real concern is about the house and children, can he refrain from smoking in the house and around the children? If so, they may have a negotiable issue. Or can they put a definite time limit on Jeff's smoking? Then they might also have a negotiable issue. If not, they may be facing a bottom line and will need to consider ending the relationship.

Bottom lines are critical. If you are not aware of your own and your partner's bottom lines, your relationship is in trouble. Good relationships are built on honesty, trust, and respect for one another. If these principles are violated, the relationship is rocky.

The Negotiations

You've got an issue you want to negotiate with your partner. It's something that's been bothering you a long time and you want to make some changes. Win-win negotiation sounds like a good method to resolve the problem. Now, how do you go about it? Where and when will you meet? What will you say? How will you handle an impasse? The following is a step-by-step guide for getting ready for the negotiation, doing it, and finalizing your agreement.

Getting Ready

The setting for any negotiation is going to have a large impact on the outcome. Labor negotiators recognize this and pay a lot of attention to the details of establishing a place for negotiations. The following suggestions may aid in promoting win-win outcomes.

1. *Set aside a time of day in which you are both bright and alert, and not preoccupied with other concerns.* Many people feel most creative in the morning.
2. *Set time parameters from the very beginning.* Know that you have, say, from 8:00 to 10:00 A.M. for this particular negotiation. To promote thorough discussion, be generous with the time you allow. If you're halfway through a negotiation and find that your time is up, it's not only frustrating, but it will take additional time to pick up from where you left off when you resume the session.
3. *Arrange a place that is quiet and free of all distractions and interruptions.* Absolutely no telephone calls, doorbells, children, burglars, or things that go bump in the night. No blaring music, television, or anything else that would divert your attention from the matter at hand. In fact, if at all possible get away from the house and meet at a neutral

area, such as a restaurant. If you decide to meet at home, take the phone off the hook and agree not to answer the doorbell if it rings.

4. *Prepare materials in advance.* Outline a proposal with some reasonable solutions that are acceptable to you. Table 1.1 illustrates such a proposal. Also prepare any factual data you may need to make an informed decision. If one of your solutions is to hire someone to come in and clean your house, you will need to have an estimate of the cost. If one of your solutions is to enroll your three-year-old in a daycare center, then you might want a list of daycare centers, locations, costs, enrollment information, and so on. You will also want to have blank paper, pencils, rulers, and calculators available for your negotiation. Pull any relevant files and keep them handy for quick reference.

Table 1.1

Proposal for Changing Arrangements for Dinner Parties

Statement of Problem: When we entertain your clients with Saturday evening dinner parties, it is a three-week effort for me. Since I have started working, I have to use my evenings and weekend time to make the arrangements, often when I'm very tired. The day of the dinner party I essentially "lose" my Saturday getting ready for the party. I am just about at my breaking point.

Proposed Options:

1. *Hire a Caterer.* With this option we could still entertain clients at home. I've checked with caterers in town and they charge from $10 to $20 per person depending on the menu. While it's difficult to put a price tag on my time and energy, I am certainly going to be happier and a lot more pleasant if I am relieved of this responsibility.

2. *Entertain at a Restaurant.* This may not be as desirable as the home atmosphere, but it would solve the problem. The costs are dependent on the restaurant. Generally they would range from $15 to $35 per person.

3. *Entertain More Casually.* Take the clients to a football or hockey game and come back for light refreshments.

4. *Fix the Dinner Yourself.* I am working full-time with many outside obligations. If you want an elegant meal at home, you could take care of it, just as you would any of your other work obligations.

Doing It—Key Strategies

Your odds for a successful session are greatly increased if you handle the negotiations properly. Some key strategies include the following:

1. *Sit side by side at a table.* This serves both a psychological and a practical purpose. Psychologically if you are sitting side by side your focus is "ahead" or toward reaching a satisfactory agreement. When people sit facing each other, they are more prone to get caught up in a confrontation. Sitting side by side is more conducive to focusing on the problem—the problem you have in front of both of you. For the sake of practicality, sitting side by side allows you to look at each other's worksheets, lists, proposals, and options. It is also easier to work on joint proposals this way.

2. *Be friendly and calm.* You are meeting to solve a problem, not to argue. You won't aid your cause by telling your partner how you've felt about living in a pig-pen for months. Nor do you need to complain about how terrible it was when the car broke down again last week; he or she undoubtedly has already heard your complaints. If your partner accepts your statement that there is a problem, then get right into the problem-solving phase of the session. If your partner tells you that there's no problem with the general state of the house or the car, then you need to relate in a calm but firm manner that you perceive a problem and you want to work out a solution. If your partner responds, "Then that's your problem, not mine," you will have to respond by saying that it is indeed a problem for both of you since it is affecting your relationship. At this point present your list of options and ask your partner to suggest options you haven't considered, or brainstorm additional options with you.

3. *Figure out your partner's needs.* Find out exactly what your partner likes and dislikes, is willing and is not willing to do, and then go for solutions that will meet both of your needs. The solution is often right there, but obscured by imprecision and misunderstanding—just like Vince who wanted to jog but really didn't care if Natalie cooked dinner or not. However, Natalie wasn't clear on this, and they had a problem until they talked it out.

   You may need to go beyond the superficial statement of the problem and probe your partner for the reasons behind a certain preference. For instance, neither you nor your partner wants to buy the groceries. You don't want to because you hate grocery shopping, period. Don't assume your partner's reason is the same. Ask him or her. You may find out your partner dislikes grocery shopping because it cuts out valuable weekend time. Or that the kids always beg for treats in the store. If that's the case, suggest a deal whereby your partner buys groceries on a weekday or evening while you take care of the kids. Exchange this for meal preparation, housework, or some other equivalent chore.

4. *Use humor to relieve tension.* Create some absolutely outrageous solution to the problem and have a good laugh. Incidentally, this technique is often useful in inspiring your creativity. Your attempts to come up with some offbeat options may trigger you to consider options that will work.

5. *Create early successes.* This is what the pros do in contract negotiations. It's pleasing and sets a good tone for the rest of the session. Let your partner know that you'll go out of your way to help solve the problem. For instance, if you're willing to buy the second-hand car with your own savings, bring that up at the beginning of the session.

6. *Learn to communicate effectively.* Several techniques for effective communication are listed in the next section of this chapter.

Finishing Up the Negotiations

Get It on Paper. After you have worked out the details of the negotiation, write out the agreement so that you can both go over it and make sure there are no misunderstandings. This is important. If you have decided to try out the new arrangement for a certain period of time, make sure that this is included and the appropriate dates entered into your calendars. Also, you may decide to reconsider the agreement at a specified time, perhaps on an annual basis. When the agreement is completely written up, make two copies so that you both can have one.

Celebrate Your Successes. Once you've found a solution that works, let your partner know how happy you are to make the change. Build in any extras that will make the system work. Use charts with gold stars. Write a note telling your partner how good you're feeling. Draw a before and after caricature of yourself. Go to a nice restaurant, buy champagne, go to a movie, go bicycling. Send roses. Enjoy your new decision, enjoy your partner, enjoy yourself!

Do's and Don'ts of Effective Communication

Effective communication is the key to successful negotiations. If you use emotionally-charged language that sets off your partner, your odds for a win-win solution are slim. Here are some guidelines to keep your minds open and your tempers mild.

1. *Never Say Never.* Avoid the use of "never" and "always" in your conversation. Statements such as, "You never pay me a compliment," or "You always drive too fast" are almost never correct and will create a defensive (not cooperative) posture in your partner.

2. *Use "I" Statements and Avoid "You" Statements.* State your thoughts without judging your partner. For example, "I would like you to tell me when you're going to work late," not "You never tell me when you're going to be late," or "I would like to share the decisions on which movies we see," not "You always decide which movie to see."

3. *Avoid "Shoulds."* "Shoulds" stir up much more trouble than they'll ever be worth. Should statements imply that you are judging your partner and that you are the authority. It's an implied parent-child "I'm right, you're wrong" position. Most of the time the use of "should" elicits a strong negative reaction, particularly if you're dealing with sensitive issues. Imagine how you'd feel if your partner said, "You should have worked with the kids on their homework so they would have gotten better grades" or "You should have made a better time in that ten-kilometer race."

4. *Avoid Insults and Sarcasm.* This is important, even if the comment is intended as a joke. For example, "I guess you like dirty bathrooms, judging from the way you clean them," or "Have you ever considered using deodorant?"

5. *Avoid Long Lectures.* Your partner likely will tune you out if you begin a long discourse on how bad the problem is. Instead, state the problem simply, in one sentence if possible. Then move on to solutions.

6. *Stick to the Subject.* If the subject happens to be about where you're going to spend the holidays, don't get sidetracked on how much you overspent your gift budget last year. Stay on the topic until it gets resolved. You can monitor both yourself and your partner and keep the discussion on target with comments such as "Let's keep on the subject here and decide where we will go at Christmas. We can discuss money issues at another session if you'd like."

7. *Don't Dwell on the Past.* You're meeting in order to change things, to make the future better, so don't itemize past events. Use present tense statements like, "It bothers me when we arrive late to teacher conferences and other meetings. I'd like your help in arriving on time for today's meeting." Notice the difference in tone with, "We've been late at every single meeting at school because of you. You don't have any respect for me or the children's teachers."

8. *Practice Reflective Listening.* This technique will ensure that you are hearing your partner accurately. Reflective listening involves restating your partner's comments in your own words. For example, you might reflect back to your partner, "It sounds like you are concerned that the children are watching television instead of doing their homework,"

or "You seem to indicate that you would like more free time on Saturdays instead of cleaning the house," or "What I'm hearing you say is that you need your own space somewhere in the house that you can use as an office."

9 . *Clarify and Summarize.* As you get into the negotiation, clarify both your position and your partner's. For example, "Are you suggesting that we set some rules about television viewing and doing homework?" or "Let's see here. You're willing to do some housework, but not on Saturdays. Is that right?" Or, "It sounds like we can work this out if we move the furniture out of the spare bedroom and get you a desk and lamp and chair. Would that work for you?"

Joint Decision Making

People tend to focus so heavily on the logical aspects of decision making that the emotional aspects are often disregarded. Both logic and emotion should be involved in the decision. Both partners should end the negotiation session feeling good about themselves individually, about their relationship, and about the decision. They should be in a frame of mind to go out and implement the decision and then get on with the rest of life's activities.

Emotional Components of Joint Decision Making

Unfortunately emotions frequently get in the way of making changes. You may find yourself facing the following:

1 . *Sadness.* There are productive tears and there are unproductive tears. You will need to develop a sensitivity to both. If your partner displays genuine sadness, it is important for those feelings to be expressed, but a negotiation session is not the appropriate place. If the flow of tears can't be stopped, reschedule the session. Then request a more dry-eyed approach at the next meeting.

2 . *Anger.* Like sadness, anger can be controlled and useful or uncontrolled and harmful. You may want to calmly make statements like, "It makes me angry when you forget to make dinner on your night." Raising your voice and using threatening language, however, can jeopardize the session. If you find that you or your partner are too angry to negotiate reasonably, call off the session and schedule another one. Before you have that next session, agree with your partner to control the anger so that it won't interfere with the problem-solving process. Take your anger out on a pillow, a tennis ball, or other inanimate object before the next session.

3 . *Fear of the Unknown.* Your partner may be reluctant to make changes in the relationship because he or she is more comfortable with a familiar situation. If this is the case, you will want your partner to focus on these fears and work out a plan together to alleviate them.

4 . *Need to Be in Control.* Some people feel a pressing need to be in control of any given situation. If they are threatened with losing some control, they are likely to resist. If you find yourself in this situation, you will need to go over the specifics of the plan with your partner indicating the overall gain by having a sharing relationship, rather than a controlling one.

Logical Components of Decision Making

Establishing a Fair System in an Unfair World. All of us have faced disadvantages. For years women and minorities have been handicapped with respect to employment opportunities. Lack of formal education has been a burden for many people. The elderly have faced discriminatory practices. The list is lengthy.

How do you handle a situation in which your partner is in a better financial position? Or has a more flexible work situation? Or is more mechanically talented? If your partner is an M.D. and you hold a bachelor's degree in elementary education, your partner's earning capacity is going to be much greater than yours. Similarly, if your partner is a college professor and you're a bank teller, your partner is going to have much more time flexibility than you. How do you resolve these differences and set up a system that is workable and fair to both of you?

There are obviously no pat answers to these questions. What you face is working out an arrangement that satisfies both of you. You will need to find options that you both believe are fair. They will differ from couple to couple. For example, John feels fine about totally supporting his three stepchildren, including putting them through college. On the other hand, Frank, who is extremely warm and loving to his two young stepdaughters, has demanded that his wife Maxine take her ex-husband to court to collect support payments.

When it comes right down to it you will have to continuously work out systems that seem fair to you. You may well need to renegotiate items like finances and housework on an annual basis. You will also want to consider how others have reached a fair and workable system. Their ideas may trigger some for you.

Steps in the Decision-Making Process. Logical decision making is based on (1) understanding yourself and your needs, (2) recognizing the resources available, (3) weighing the consequences of the various options available, (4) going with the best decision given the information available.

While this seems concise and easy, it isn't. Information is frequently not available, resources may be extremely limited, and no one decision or set of decisions may come leaping out as the best. However, once you've made the decision, allow time to reflect on it. Possibly new information will come up or you may get a clearer grasp of your feelings or objections. If so, schedule a time to meet with your partner and go over the new information.

Hammers and Nails

Several decision-making tools may be useful in making difficult decisions with your partner. These range from simple pro and con lists to more complex decision matrices with weighted rankings. Most of these tools are borrowed from management science where decisions are made with as much objectivity as possible. You will, of course, need to consider emotion in your decisions. After some experimentation you will probably find a method which is most comfortable and useful. If one method is not particularly helpful, try another. But remember you are ultimately responsible for your decision. These are merely tools to aid you in the process.

Pro and Con List

This is a popular and useful method for clarifying or evaluating a particular decision. Many people find this method sufficient for their purposes and rarely need more complicated methods. The mechanics are straightforward. At the top of a piece of paper write out the proposal you are considering—to buy a personal computer, to build an addition to your house, to start a consulting business. In one column list all the reasons in favor of the action, and in another column list all the reasons against the action. Doing this jointly is a good idea; your partner may come up with some reasons you may have missed or forgotten. After you have completed the list, discuss it with your partner.

One caution: keep in mind that certain items, either pro or con, may be more meaningful than others. Don't equate each pro with each con and simply base the decision on the longest list.

If after your discussion neither of you is leaning in one direction or the other, I would suggest that you sleep on it and come back to it later, or use another method of evaluation.

Table 1.2 is an example of a couple using a pro and con list to decide whether to purchase a larger home.

Table 1.2

Pro and Con List

Mary and Don's Considerations for Buying a Larger House

Pro	Con
We need more space; we're cramped now and that will get worse as the kids grow up. It would be good to get established in a neighborhood before the children start school.	We would be pretty strapped financially for about a year or two. No big vacations or new cars.
We probably could sell our current house without much difficulty in the summer months.	Even though interest rates are lower than they have been, we would still be paying significantly higher interest than on our current house.
Interest rates are a little better now than they have been in a while.	We would not be able to afford new furnishings for a few years, and then we would only be able to furnish the house modestly.
We are both doing well in our current jobs, so there is every indication to believe our financial situation will steadily improve.	

Force Field Analysis

A force field analysis is somewhat more sophisticated than a pro and con list in that it requires you to look at both the positives and negatives of a particular decision, then to list the ways in which you can strengthen the positive forces and overcome the negative forces impinging on the decision. Frequently specific action steps with deadlines are added.

Table 1.3 illustrates the use of a force field analysis.

Rank Ordering

Sometimes examining the positives and negatives can put you into a quandary. The pros may be balanced out by the cons. Or there may be several pros, and one big, overwhelming con. In cases like this, the rank ordering method may be useful. Simply list each option in your own order of preference. Then compare your list with your partner's. This method serves to make you more aware of your values and forces a decision (and discussion) as to why you value one option over another.

Table 1.3

Force Field Analysis
Should Marybeth Go Back to Work?

Step One.   *State the Problem:*

Marybeth is trying to decide whether to go back to work after having been home with small children for eight years. She wants to work, but isn't sure if it's the right decision for her family.

Step Two.   *List the Positive Forces Supporting the Decision:*

1. I liked working before having children.
2. I get bored at home.
3. We need the second income.
4. The children are both in school and don't need me as much.

Step Three.   *List the Negative Forces that Hinder the Decision:*

1. There wouldn't be anyone to take care of things at home.
2. There would be lots of extra chores for everyone.
3. There might be a problem finding before and after school childcare.
4. There would be little time for children's carpools, bakesales, PTA, etc.
5. Who would take over in emergencies?

Step Four.   *List the Actions You Can Take to Strengthen the Positive Forces from Step Two:*

1. I could look for an interesting, people-oriented job.
2. I could look for a job with good salary potential.
3. I could teach the children to be independent in more situations.

Step Five.   *List the Actions You Can Take to Reduce the Negative Forces from Step Three:*

1. We could have a family meeting and divide up the chores.
2. We could hire someone to help with the housework.
3. We could lower the standards for the housework.
4. We could teach the children how to do more chores.
5. I could ask other working mothers in the neighborhood how they handle childcare. I could get names and phone numbers of potential sitters before starting work.
6. Hal could take over the carpools and emergencies until I get situated in a new job.

Table 1.4

Rank Order Method

Marge and Ben's Choice for Wedding Music

Marge	Ben
1. Handel's *Water Music*	1. Blake's hymn "Jerusalem"
2. Pachelbel's *Canon*	2. Campra's *Triumphal March*
3. Jeremiah Clarke's *Trumpet Voluntary*	3. Handel's *Water Music*
4. Haydn's *Serenade*	4. Pachelbel's *Canon*
5. Beethoven's Minuet in G	5. Simon and Garfunkle's "Bridge Over Troubled Waters"
6. Beethoven's *Für Elise*	6. Aaron Copeland's "Fanfare to the Common Man"

The discussion: Because there was some overlap, Marge and Ben decided to use selections from *Water Music*, Pachelbel's *Canon*, "Jerusalem," and *Trumpet Voluntary*. They decided to use Campra's *Triumphal March* as the recessional, and to play "Bridge Over Troubled Waters" at the reception.

Report Card

The report card method is particularly useful in evaluating two or more items when you have several criteria to consider. When using this method, list all your criteria in one column and compare each of the alternatives you are considering against each criterion. Then give each a rating from A to E or one to five. You may want to save space for comments, too. Couples may use this method by each making a separate report card and later comparing notes, or by jointly putting together a composite evaluation.

Table 1.5 is an example of a composite report card.

Weighted Order Decision Matrix

The weighted order decision matrix is a step beyond the report card method. Its particular usefulness is in giving more weight to the more important considerations.

Table 1.6 illustrates the use of the weighted order decision matrix. In this example Don and Mary decided to lump together all of their considerations into three main groupings: house characteristics (size and quality of rooms, conditions, etc.), finances (price, terms, taxes, etc.), and location (neighborhood, schools, noise, etc.). Then they decided that the house characteristics were more important than the financing and location. They decided to give the house characteristics a weight of three, and finances

Table 1.5

Report Card Method—Don and Mary's Evaluation of Three Potential Houses

Criteria	House A		House B		House C		Comments
	Don	Mary	Don	Mary	Don	Mary	
Financial							
Price	A	A	B	B	C	C	Clear cut prices. House A
Terms	A	A	B	B	B	B	is considerably less
Taxes	A	A	B	B	C	C	Than B+C.
Utilities	A	A	A	A	B	B	
Location							
Nice Neighborhood	A	A	B	B	A	A	Both B+C in good neighborhoods.
Proximity to Work	C	B	C	B	B	C	Mary would have a long commute
Proximity to Shopping	A	A	A	A	A	A	with house C.
Proximity to Friends	B	B	B	B	A	A	
School System	C	C	B	B	A	A	School for house A has poor reputation.
Street Noise & Traffic	C	D	A	A	A	A	House A on busy street.
House Characteristics							
Lot Size and Yard	C	C	A	B	A	A	House C has big yard.
Structurally Sound	C	C	A	A	A	A	
Living Room	B	C	B	B	A	A	
Family Room	NONE	NONE	NONE	NONE	A	A	
Kitchen	C	D-E	B	C	A	A	House A has tiny kitchen.
Dining Room	B	D-E	B	C	A	A	
Bathrooms	B	C	B	B	A	A	
Master Bedroom	C	C	B	B	A	A	House C has beautiful master bedroom.
Other Bedrooms	B	C	B	C	A	A	
Basement	D	C	C	C	A	A	House A has a damp cellar.
Garage	NONE	NONE	A	A	A	A	
Storage Space	D	C	A	A	A	A	

Table 1.6

Weighted Order Decision Matrix
Don and Mary's Evaluation of Potential House

Evaluation Criteria	House A		House B		House C		Comments
	Don	Mary	Don	Mary	Don	Mary	
House Characteristics	5	3	7	5	10	10	Evaluated on a Scale of 1 (low) to 10 (high).
Finances	10	10	7	8	6	6	Don and Mary individually evaluated each house and recorded it.
Location	6	5	7	8	10	8	

Scoring

Add individual scores for each house's evaluation criteria, and multiply by weight.

House Characteristics are weighted 3; Finances 2; and Location 1. Add totals for each house.

	House A	House B	House C
House Characteristics (weighted 3)	$5 + 3 = 8$ $8 \times 3 = 24$	$7 + 5 = 12$ $12 \times 3 = 36$	$10 + 10 = 20$ $20 \times 3 = 60$
Finances (weighted 2)	$10 + 10 = 20$ $20 \times 2 = 40$	$7 + 8 = 15$ $15 \times 2 = 30$	$6 + 6 = 12$ $12 \times 2 = 24$
Locations (weighted 1)	$6 + 5 = 11$	$7 + 8 = 15$	$10 + 8 = 18$
TOTALS	75	81	102

House C is ahead with 102.

a weight of two, and location a weight of one. Then they each evaluated the three groups: house characteristics, finances, and location, and rated them on a one (low) to ten (high) scale. After multiplying each rating by its weight, they compiled the totals. Looking at the totals they discussed their individual ratings and the reasons for their choices.

Using Counselors

If you are both sincerely motivated in your attempts to better your relationship but are having trouble doing it on your own, then you may want to consult a counselor. A counselor will not be able to "save" your relationship, but he or she can contribute in several ways. First, a counselor will be able to assess if both of you are really willing to make changes, and if so, help identify the obstacles in your way. Second, a counselor can aid you in the communication process and can suggest new methods for "neutralizing" the information flow. Third, a counselor can aid in adjusting the balance of power in the relationship. This is especially important if there has been an imbalance for some time.

Counselors vary widely in their training. Some are social workers, some are psychologists, some are psychiatrists with M.D. degrees, and some have no particular credentials. State laws vary considerably. Obviously they will have very different styles and approaches depending on their backgrounds and experience. As a prospective client you will need to be very selective to insure finding someone who will work effectively with you.

Table 1.7 lists criteria you will want to consider when selecting a counselor. You should be able to determine answers to most or all of these questions after one session with a counselor. Because the costs are often a concern (or excuse for not going), be sure and check about sliding scales, insurance coverage, and other cost-related policies. Most communities have low-cost mental health agencies which offer counseling services, also.

The Male-Female Counseling Team

You may want to consider a male-female counseling team when deciding on counselors. Besides the obvious benefit of two professionals helping you, the team is useful in providing both male and female perspectives to an issue. A team can offer a more balanced approach with more room for empathy on particular topics. The synergistic effect of two people also can add to the creativity needed to solve many complex issues.

Table 1.7

Counselor Selection Criteria

1. What are the counselor's credentials? Education? Specialized training? Years of experience?

2. Does the counselor have a pleasing personality and a good sense of humor? Do you feel comfortable with him or her?

3. Does the counselor treat you as an equal without a condescending attitude?

4. Will the counselor try new approaches if the old ones are not getting anywhere? Ask him or her to give examples.

5. Does the counselor make sense and seem to understand your situation? Does he or she use clear and understandable language?

6. Is the counselor himself or herself in an intimate primary relationship and willing to discuss it?

7. Is the counselor clear about fees, insurance coverage, and related matters?

Recommended Reading

Broderick, Carlfred B. *Couples: How to Confront Problems and Maintain Loving Relationships.* New York: Simon and Schuster, 1978.

Fisher, Roger and William Ury. *Getting to Yes.* Boston: Houghton Mifflin Co., 1981.

Kimball, Gayle. *The 50/50 Marriage.* Boston: Beacon Press, 1983.

Siegelman, Ellen Y. *Personal Risk.* New York: Harper & Row, 1983.

Warschaw, Tessa Albert. *Winning by Negotiation.* New York: Berkley Books, 1980.

Wheeler, Daniel D. and Irving L. Janis. *A Practical Guide for Making Decisions.* New York: The Free Press, 1980.

2

Lifestyle:
Mr. and Ms., Miss, or Mrs.

Who walks the dog? Who makes dinner on Sunday? Who pays for the HBO movie channel? While these questions all need answers if you want a smoothly running household, they ignore the broader lifestyle questions—questions which determine the pace and quality of life. Lifestyle questions go beneath the surface of *how* to do something and look at *whether* to do it. Shall we even own a dog—or any pet? Shall we have a Sunday dinner—or any evening meal? Shall we purchase the movie channel—or even own a television?

Lifestyle questions originate with our value systems and are concerned with how we choose to live. Individual lifestyle questions include the following: Is an intimate, primary relationship important to me? Is having children part of my life goals? Do I view my job merely as a source of income or also as a means of achieving recognition and personal satisfaction? Do I want to be free to pick up and move across the country on a moment's notice? Or do I want to establish roots in a stable environment?

These kinds of lifestyle questions need to be posed as individual soul-searching questions in order to set up individual goals and get a sense of personal direction. They are also important, however, as relationship questions. Do the two of you share similar values and life goals? Is there room for reconciliation and compromise in the areas in which you differ? How do the two of you prioritize these questions?

A commonality of values is critical in establishing a long-lasting intimate relationship. You undoubtedly will have difficulty working out your differences if you want children and your partner doesn't, if you want sexual freedom and your partner doesn't, if you think money is to be saved and your partner doesn't, if you want your popcorn buttered and your partner doesn't.

Table 2.1, Values Clarification, may help you get started in sorting out your individual priorities and provide a starting point for discussion with your partner. As you discuss these terms, be sure to define what each one means to you. For instance, a high ranking on "education" need not mean you want to spend six more years in school, but simply to be well-read and participate in scholarly discussions. "Income" will take on different meanings from person to person; what is sufficient for one person, may not be for another. "Parenthood" may mean ten children to one person and a cockapoo to another.

Table 2.1

Values Clarification

Rank order each of the following terms. Compare your ranking with your partner's ranking. Discuss what each term means to you.

Aesthetics	To have beautiful surroundings.
Education	To become a well-educated person.
Esteem	To be recognized and highly regarded by others.
Fitness	To stay fit through regular exercise and proper diet.
Income	To make considerable money.
Independence	To be free to do and say as I choose.
Parenthood	To have children and share a part of their development.
Power	To have much influence and authority over others.
Relationship	To have a close, primary relationship with someone I love.
Religion	To worship and live by my beliefs.
Security	To be secure in my job, relationship, and my environment.
Service	To aid in the welfare of others.
Social Acceptance	To be liked by others.

Basic Choices: Living Together or Marriage

One basic question you and your partner face is the kind of commitment you want to have with each other. This may range from the couple who chooses separate residences, separate friends, and separate lovers, to the couple who chooses a traditional long-term marriage. For most people, however, it will be somewhere in between, with an agreement to have an intimate, primary relationship either living together or married.

Nevertheless, even within the context of cohabitation (living together) or marriage there is a wide variety of choices. These include where you choose to live and how you choose to live.

Whether you consider cohabitation as an option is likely to depend on its acceptance in your community and whether you have role models of others choosing that lifestyle. Your idea of what constitutes a marriage, similarly, will be colored by the marriages of your friends and relatives. Whether you consider a commuter relationship with each of you maintaining separate residences will depend again on social expectations and role models as well as career demands and finances.

If you are considering either cohabitation or marriage, the following questions may be useful in clarifying pertinent issues.

1. How do you view your commitment to each other? What are the positive aspects? The negative aspects?
2. How long do you plan to stay together?
3. What kind of sexual relationship do you want? Is it to be monogamous?
4. What kind of financial arrangement do you want? How are you going to keep track of finances?
5. What kind of housekeeping arrangements do you want?
6. How much time do you plan to spend together? On a daily basis? On a weekly basis?
7. Do you plan to have separate friendships, hobbies, and vacations?
8. Do you want children? If so, when and how many?
9. How do you plan to celebrate special holidays?
10. How will you evaluate if the arrangement is working out? If you decide to split up, how will you go about it? How will you handle the logistics, e.g., house, car, pets?

Living Together

While researchers have thoroughly examined the institution of marriage and its dramatic changes over the past few years, only sketchy information exists about unmarried couples who choose to live together. We do know that cohabitation is rapidly increasing in this country. The 1981 population survey indicated that there were about 1.8 million unmarried couples living together in the United States.[1]

What accounts for this dramatic increase in cohabitation over the past few years? We can speculate a few reasons: (1) Changing morals have made it socially acceptable. (2) There is a growing skepticism of marriage which has been exacerbated by the skyrocketing divorce rate. (3) Many couples are using it as a relationship test or trial marriage.

When considering cohabitation as a lifestyle option, you should take into consideration the community in which you plan to live. It may not be looked on favorably in a small, conservative town. Also recognize that not all employers or relatives will favor this type of arrangement. On the other hand, you will probably find that cohabitation is widely accepted in the larger metropolitan areas. Observe your circle of friends and acquaintances. If they're living together without facing social stigma, chances are good you could, too.

One popular belief is that cohabitation keeps you outside the legal system, and therefore has advantages over marriage. You have separate tax forms, no joint property, no need for a divorce if you break up. It sounds very appealing to many couples—especially those who have been through painful divorce proceedings.

But be cautious. This may not always be true. The famous court case of Michelle Triola against actor Lee Marvin illustrated that the legal system, may, in fact, recognize the legitimacy of such an arrangement. While "palimony" is not awarded every day, this case reflects a recognition that cohabitation is widespread, socially acceptable, and subject to the vagaries of the legal system. If you choose to live together, don't make any assumptions about your legal status. If you have questions, consult an attorney.

Another aspect of cohabitation that couples find attractive is that it gives them a certain amount of distance from each other. They indicate that it's important for each of them to maintain a separate identity; they view marriage as fusing them too closely together. By remaining unmarried they can each be themselves—not a wife or husband of someone else. They keep their own names, jobs, property, savings, and debts.

Of course, this needn't be the case. Cohabiting couples may develop very dependent relationships and married couples may have very independent ones. Like so many other things, it's a matter of perception. If you think you'll feel more independent living together than married, chances are you'll be more independent. Similarly, if you think you'd be unhappy living together, chances are you'd be unhappy. If you think you'd be wildly ecstatic living together that might even happen, too.

Getting Married

Today marriage is a vastly different institution than it was a few decades ago. With 50 percent of current marriages ending in divorce, marriage is no longer a till-death-do-us-part commitment. For some couples this high divorce rate means the opportunity to leave a relationship that isn't working—for whatever reason. This new freedom to leave can mean that couples give up potentially good relationships because one or both partners isn't willing to weather the rough periods.

For couples who have lived together, marriage may not feel any different than living together. Many people, however, report feeling a psychological difference. They usually describe this difference in the strength of their commitment—marriage means putting an extra effort into maintaining the relationship and working toward being part of the 50 percent of marriages that do survive.

Marriage also offers social acceptance. This may be of primary importance to those couples wanting to have children. While cohabitation in many areas has become socially acceptable for childless couples, it has not been popularly accepted for childbearing couples. Marriage is still the norm.

Marriage also has certain legal consequences involving joint property and responsibilities. If you have questions regarding legal concerns, by all means consult an attorney.

Unfortunately couples frequently mention that they do not have any positive role models for marriage—particularly if their parents did not have good marriages. Your marriage doesn't have to resemble that of your parents (although without conscious effort, it likely will). Nor does your marriage have to look like those on television or in the movies. While Jackie Gleason's "Honeymooners" makes great entertainment even today, Ralph and Alice Kramden are no role models for marriage. If you recognize that marriage is more than a societal expectation and the convenience of having a husband to take out the garbage and a wife to sew on buttons, you can make it a positive commitment to many years of shared experiences. For those who choose marriage, the options are plentiful. Just ask those who have experienced good marriages—they will have many useful insights.

Hoboken or Hamtramck: Where You Choose to Live

Frequently people do not make an active decision regarding the part of the country in which they want to live. Either they settle down near the place they grew up or they accept a job that requires a particular location. It may be advantageous to live near your family and you may want to hang onto a good job, but you may be short-sighted if you do not consider any other factors when choosing a place to live.

Places Rated Almanac, an excellent resource for this subject, uses nine basic criteria for judging 277 metropolitan areas in the country. The criteria are climate and terrain, housing, health care and environment, crime, transportation, education, recreation, arts, and economics.[2]

Climate and terrain refers to such items as average temperature and humidity, amount of snowfall, rainfall, number of sunny days. It also includes bad weather occurrences such as frequency of hailstorms, hurricanes, and tornadoes. These factors may be very important to you if you work outside or tend to spend much of your leisure time outdoors.

Housing factors include average single-family house prices, property tax, and energy requirements (heat and air-conditioning costs). Health care and environment includes information such as geographic patterns of disease.

Health care facilities are judged by number of physicians and hospital beds per resident. Also included are factors such as the availability of teaching hospitals, medical schools, HMOs, and specialized health centers.

In assessing crime, the *Places Rated Almanac* uses factors the FBI has linked to local crime rates to determine safe and dangerous places to live. These factors include (1) population density; (2) composition of the population, e.g., age and sex; (3) economic status—particularly job availability; (4) cultural conditions; (5) population stability; (6) climate; (7) strength of police force; (8) policies and attitudes of judicial system; and (9) community attitudes toward crime.[3]

Transportation includes airport ratings, railroad ratings, traffic patterns, mass transit systems. Education includes ratings of, among others, student-teacher ratios, teacher salaries, and national test scores.

Recreation includes availability of public golf courses, bowling, public parks, movie theaters, bars, zoos, aquariums, amusement parks, professional sports, race tracks, and ski areas. The arts refers to symphonies, opera companies, dance, theater, public television, museums, and libraries. Economics includes fiscal factors such as bond ratings, average household income, taxes, unemployment averages, and expected job growth.

Depending on your professional and personal interests, you would probably view some of these factors as more important than others. If you have no children and have completed your own formal education, then education might be of little interest. But if water sports are a big part of your life, climate and recreation would be important considerations. If you have allergies, environmental issues and climate would be a concern.

In making a decision about where to live, it may be helpful to make up a matrix, either individually or jointly with your partner. Table 2.2 illustrates a weighted order matrix which Suzanne and Craig drew up based on their individual and joint needs and interests.

Table 2.2

Suzanne and Craig's Ranking of Places to Live

Weighted Order Method   1 = Worst   5 = Best

	Nashville TN	Miami FL	Boulder CO	Albuquerque NM	Austin TX
Evaluation Criteria					
Colleges and Universities	3	3	5	4	5
Housing Costs	4	1	2	2	4
Ski Areas	1	1	5	5	1
Movie Theaters	5	5	5	5	5
Proximity to Parents in Texas	3	3	1	1	5

Scoring

Multiply ranking by weight. Add totals for each city.

	Nashville TN	Miami FL	Boulder CO	Albuquerque NM	Austin TX
Colleges and Universities Weighted 3	3(x3)=9	3(x3)=9	5(x3)=15	4(x3)=12	5(x3)=15
Housing Costs Weighted 2	4(x2)=8	1(x2)=2	2(x2)=4	2(x2)=4	4(x2)=8
Ski Areas Weighted 1	1	1	5	5	1
Movie Theaters Weighted 1	5	5	5	5	5
Proximity to Parents in Texas Weighted 1	3	3	1	1	5
Totals	26	20	30	27	34

Austin is highest with 34; Boulder is next with 30.

In this table the couple took the five cities where Craig had good job opportunities and used them as a basis to start the ratings. Suzanne's first criterion was college, since she had two and one-half years to finish. Next in importance was housing costs. Then they added ski sites and movie theaters—their favorite forms of recreation. They also included accessibility to parents (both sets live in the Dallas-Fort Worth area).

The couple rated the places on a scale of one to five, one being the worst and five being the best. They decided to weigh college three times as heavily, and housing costs twice as heavily as the other criteria. Boulder and Austin emerged as the best choices given their criteria. As it turned out, the job offer in Austin was somewhat better, so they decided on Austin, with the plan that they would re-evaluate their situation after Suzanne finished college.

Specific Housing Considerations

Besides the general geographical location, you and your partner will need to decide on other specifics regarding housing. Do you want to live in a rural or urban environment? Do you want to rent or buy or build? Do you prefer a new or older building? What kind of neighborhood do you prefer? How far are you willing to commute to your job? How close do you wish to be located to grocery stores, retail establishments, banks, and restaurants? How close do you want to be to schools? Or hospitals? Do you want a neighborhood that's safe for jogging? Are there swimming pools or health facilities nearby? These are all decisions you will need to ponder with your partner before making a move. In one way or another they all determine and shape your lifestyle.

How You Want to Live

Your source of income will most likely be the major determinant of your lifestyle. Not only does your job determine your earnings, but also it determines your time flexibility and leisure, and in large part, your power and status. The amount of physical challenge, risk-taking, and excitement in your job also affects your lifestyle. So does the actual environment in which you work—be it in a hospital, on a road repair crew, in a bank, or on an assembly line.

The amount of social interaction on the job and the pace of your work also influences the type of lifestyle which you choose to complement your work activities. If you spend eight hours a day at a computer terminal, you may find that you are in need of lots of social interaction during your non-work hours. Or, if you work in sales, meeting people on a continual basis, you may find yourself seeking out much time alone during non-work hours.

Determining what work values are most important to you will help you clarify what types of jobs and career paths will best suit your personality. The Work Values Clarification Table in chapter 4 may be helpful in sorting out these priorities. You may want to compare your ratings with your partner's. If you find that there are many dissimilarities, you may want to schedule some time with your partner to discuss them.

If you are not satisfied with your job and the resultant lifestyle, you may want to find a new job or consider changing careers. Chapter 4 offers several resources to aid you in this process. It is critical that you not feel stuck in any one job—for whatever reason—age, sex, handicap, lack of education, or certification. It may take some time to make a career change, but the long-term benefits may well be worth it.

Yoga, Yogurt, and Other Routes to Good Health

How you feel is a critical factor in improving and maintaining the quality of your relationship. Feeling alert, alive, and full of energy is necessary for a long-term, joyous, and growing relationship. It's also essential to a fulfilling sexual relationship. This means a commitment to fitness and health as part of your lifestyle choices.

High on your list of priorities should be a lifestyle which promotes a holistic approach to health—including proper body weight, nutrition, sleep habits, and aerobic exercise. Also, avoiding smoking, drugs, and excessive drinking will contribute to your general health and life expectancy.

Many excellent books are available which prescribe an overall approach to health and lifestyle. Several are included in the Recommended Reading section at the end of this chapter. What these books emphasize is the need to view health issues in a total perspective, which includes emotional and stress issues along with physiological factors. For instance, it is unwise to ignore recurring minor ailments such as headaches, fatigue, and indigestion. These are signals that all is not well with your physical and/or mental health. These ailments may be contributing to more major problems which could surface later on.

Also, many couples use health issues to distance themselves from each other. Rather than confronting a problem or letting themselves be intimate, they use health as an excuse. "I don't want to talk about it now, I have a headache." "I can't go with you, my back is aching." "Not tonight, dear, I'm too tired."

Using relaxation techniques such as yoga, progressive relaxation, or meditation will also promote good health. Most adult and community education programs as well as local Y's offer such classes. These techniques frequently aid in reducing stress and help you to sleep better and to feel better generally. A good massage may have the same effect.

Similarly, paying attention to what (and how much) you eat can vastly improve how you feel. If you reduce or eliminate refined sugar, salt, and caffeine, and cut down on the amount of red meat and fat in your diet, replacing these foods with high fiber grains, and fresh fruits and vegetables, not only are you less susceptible to many diseases, but you'll also feel better on a day-to-day basis.

Following an aerobic exercise program is another means of promoting good health. Whatever form of exercise you choose, you are likely to look and feel better. You should consult your physician before starting such a program, and then follow a progressive schedule which allows you to build up pace from week to week. Dr. Kenneth H. Cooper has thoroughly researched various aerobic exercises and provides programs based on a point system in his several books on aerobics. These programs allow you to choose your sport, such as swimming, walking, or bicycling, and build points based on the time and distance you exercise. This allows you to vary your choice of exercise or combine several to give you the minimum point value needed to maintain a healthful regimen.

Laughter Rediscovered

The experts are only now discovering what everyone else has known for centuries—that laughter is an important part of the human experience. Laughter is good for the mind and good for the body. In the book *Anatomy of an Illness as Perceived by the Patient*, Norman Cousins describes how he cured himself of an "irreversible" terminal disease of the connective tissue. Part of Cousins's regimen was laughter therapy—he would watch humorous movies and television programs, and read funny books in order to promote laughter. He spent lots of time watching Marx Brothers films and "Candid Camera" tapes. Cousins removed himself from the hospital environment and treated himself in the healthiest manner he thought possible, and it worked for him.

Since Cousins's book was published in 1979, a number of other books on the medical implications of laughter have emerged. There is a healing power to humor, it seems, which relieves us of the stress and tension in our bodies. In *Laugh After Laugh*, Raymond A. Moody, Jr., M.D. examines this healing process from a medical perspective. In a different vein, *The Laughter Prescription*, by Dr. Laurence J. Peter, author of *The Peter Principle*, offers practical and humorous advice for building laughter into your daily life. He offers techniques for learning how to be humorous, writing your own jokes, and incorporating humor into conversations and formal speeches. He even suggests how the communication process is facilitated through the use of humor.

Emotional Issues

If you or your partner suffer bouts of depression or other emotional disorders, it is important to seek professional help. While everyone has bad days now and then, it is essential that you feel good about yourself, your partner, and your relationship. Only this mindset can promote a win-win relationship. A positive attitude will go a long way in aiding you to reach your goals and in working out problems with your partner. Chapter 1 provides guidelines for choosing a counselor or therapist.

Making Lifestyle Changes

Changing your lifestyle may not be easy. Established patterns are difficult to break. Frequently, even if it's a small change, you'll find yourself almost automatically reverting to the old habit, particularly when under stress. Implementing a new routine requires concentration and stamina, until the new routine, in turn, becomes the established pattern.

When Peggy and Joe decided to become vegetarians, they both found grocery shopping and meal preparation much more demanding of their time and energy. "We were used to shopping and cooking in a certain way," states Peggy. "When we we switched to a vegetarian diet, we both had to think about food in a new way and it took longer. Now that we've been on the new diet for a year, it has become more routine. I now can go to the grocery store and automatically reach for the tofu and tamari where I used to reach for the hamburger and ketchup."

Relationship changes may be even more difficult—in part because we expect our partners to be mind readers. It's just possible your partner doesn't know that (1) you'd like him to give you gifts unexpectedly and for no particular reason; (2) you'd like her to take you away on a mysterious weekend trip; (3) you'd like him to initiate lovemaking in the middle of the night when you're asleep.

If you don't communicate your needs and desires, there's a fair chance you won't get them. If you decide that you want to make some lifestyle changes, by all means enlist your partner's support. If you decide to take up jogging, ask him to encourage you or even join you. If you decide to look for a different job, ask her to discuss the options with you. If you decide to lose ten pounds ask him to encourage you.

Similarly, when making joint decisions affecting lifestyle, support each other. If you choose to have an abortion, you'll need much emotional support from each other as well as from close friends. If you both decide to quit your jobs and start a catering business, it will be important to encourage each other. If you decide to build an airplane in your garage, you'd better be willing to park your car in the driveway for a few months.

Some changes are emotionally difficult. All require an up-front decision. All are going to be easier as a joint, rather than an individual, effort.

Recommended Reading

Bloomfield, Harold H., M.D. and Robert B. Kory. *The Holistic Way to Health and Happiness.* New York: Simon and Schuster, 1978.

Boyer, Richard and David Savageau. *Places Rated Almanac.* Chicago: Rand McNally & Co., 1981.

Cooper, Kenneth H., M.D. *The Aerobics Program for Total Well-Being.* New York: M. Evans and Company, 1982.

Cousins, Norman. *Anatomy of an Illness as Perceived by the Patient.* New York: W.W. Norton & Co., 1979.

Elrick, Harold, M.D.; James Crakes, Ph.D.; and Sam Clarke, M.S. *Living Longer and Better.* Mountain View, Calif.: World Publications, 1978.

McCamy, John C., M.D. and James Presley. *Human Life Styling.* New York: Harper & Row, 1975.

Moody, Raymond A., Jr., M.D. *Laugh After Laugh.* Jacksonville, Fla.: Headwaters Press, 1978.

Peter, Dr. Laurence J. and Bill Dana. *The Laughter Prescription.* New York: Ballantine Books, 1982.

Williams, Robert L. and James D. Long. *Toward a Self-managed Life Style.* Boston: Houghton Mifflin Company, 1983.

Footnotes

[1]Philip Blumstein, Ph.D. and Pepper Schwartz, Ph.D., *American Couples* (New York: William Morrow and Company, Inc., 1983), p. 36.

[2]Richard Boyer and David Savageau, *Places Rated Almanac* (Chicago: Rand McNally & Company, 1981).

[3]Ibid., pp. 137–142.

3

Personal Finances:
50-50 May Not Be a Fair Shake

Money may not be the root of all evil, but it certainly is at the heart of many broken relationships. Money is such an emotionally-laden issue that many individuals simply avoid the subject. Women, in particular, tend to back off the issue and frequently have difficulty with salary negotiations and other situations involving money. Many men experience the same qualms.

After several years of counseling couples in therapy, Bill and I have found that money is often a primary issue, particularly if a couple takes a win-lose attitude. *It is extremely important to the health of a relationship that both parties view financial decision making as a joint endeavor. They must work together to establish a fair system with some common goals.* Also, both must end up feeling good about the financial arrangement they have made, and they must feel free to initiate discussion at a later date in order to renegotiate any parts of the arrangement.

Several decisions regarding personal finances need to be made at the outset. They are itemized in Table 3.1.

All of the decisions listed are major decisions and should be reached jointly through discussion and negotiation. The specific techniques described in chapter 1 may be used. Or you may choose simply to discuss the issues until you come to a mutual decision. When difficult issues present themselves, such as decisions regarding a major purchase, a weighted order matrix (described in chapter 1) may be helpful.

No real decisions regarding personal finances can be made until one's choice of lifestyle and living arrangements are determined. Chapter 2 presents some basic considerations. They include the following: What are your long-term commitments to each other? Will you marry? Will you have children?

Table 3.1

Major Areas of Decision Making for Personal Finances

1. *Lifestyle Decisions.* Considerations for lifestyle decisions are described in chapter 2. Mutual decisions must be reached regarding (a) the cost of that lifestyle and (b) the sources of income to support that lifestyle.

2. *Mutual Agreement on a Household Budget.* A format for a household budget is provided in this chapter.

3. *Choice of Shared Financing Method.* Three methods are discussed in this chapter. You may choose to modify one to fit your specific situation. Along with this decision is the choice of separate or joint checking accounts, credit cards, loans, savings, and investments.

4. *Record-Keeping and Taxes.* This includes a method of keeping accurate and accessible records and receipts.

5. *Priorities for Major Purchases and Discretionary Income.* This includes items such as automobiles, furniture, large appliances, as well as vacations, savings, and investments.

6. *Mutual Agreement on a Long-Range Financial Plan.* This involves forecasting your financial situation on a multi-year basis. It includes decisions regarding insurance, wills, and savings. It also may include consulting experts for advice.

Do you plan to share your personal property with each other? How much income do you expect over the next few years? How do you plan to spend your income? What kinds of changes in lifestyle do you anticipate? How do you make decisions regarding time-money trade-offs?

Because housing always represents a substantial financial commitment, that decision needs careful attention. Other critical areas include career issues for both partners, long-range salary expectations, and the probability that one or both partners would drop out of the labor force for a significant length of time. These career-related issues are covered in chapter 4.

Your Household Budget

After making the initial decision regarding living arrangements and lifestyle, a natural second step involves a mutual decision regarding a household budget. It can be put together on a weekly, monthly, or yearly basis. Table 3.2, the Household Budget Form, can be used to get started.

Table 3.2
Household Budget Form

Housing	*Food/Household*
Mortgage or rent	Groceries
Home insurance	Meals out
Fuel bills	Household expenses
Telephone	Furnishings
Electricity/gas	Appliances
Water	
Real estate tax	*Non-Material*
House repairs	Education/tuition
	Medical/dental/optical
Transportation	Life/health insurance
Car payments	Childcare
Car insurance	Charities
Gasoline	Income tax
Car repairs/maintenance	
	Recreation
Personal	Vacations
Clothing	Memberships
Personal care	Entertainment
Hobbies	
	Savings
Miscellaneous	*Loans*

It may be eye-opening for both of you to do a budget projection separately and later compare notes. There may be vast discrepancies in expectations for items such as vacations or savings. You can begin negotiating priorities when consolidating these separate budgets. With this process, the areas of trade-off can be clearly recognized.

It is especially important when negotiating a household budget to be realistic and not to inflate any item in order to create a bargaining position. Remember that you want to end up with a budget that is mutually satisfactory, not one that just meets your own needs. When working on the budget, take into consideration what the previous costs have been in each area. If the newly-budgeted amount is significantly higher or lower, decide what changes in your lifestyle will be necessary to stay within the budget. Also, it might be wise to keep the items which are listed under "Personal" (e.g., clothing, cosmetics, hobbies) as a separate budget item in each individual's discretionary fund.

Always consider the emotional impact of your decisions. If you choose not to take a vacation in the upcoming year in order to save money, consider the price of that decision on your mental health. Would forgoing a vacation result in increased stress or a stress-related illness? If so, would a low-cost vacation be a better all-around decision?

In negotiating a household budget, also consider that nebulous item "Other" or, in its longer version "Miscellaneous." Because I am an optimist, I have trouble with this category. I usually think of myself as immune from accidents and unexpected expenses. However, my bubble was burst after a succession of three toothaches—each one resulting in root canal work at the cost of $600 apiece. My case may seem extreme, but be aware that misfortune does strike even in the best of circumstances.

Also build into the budget an ample allowance for automobile repairs, appliance replacements, and large home repairs such as replacing the roof or furnace. These expenses may not come up in any given year, but it is important to build in a buffer to handle them if necessary.

After setting up a household budget, any couple living together will need to work out a budgeting method for sharing the finances. Three are listed below which can be modified to your own personal circumstances.

Three Methods of Shared Financing

The Shared Wealth/Shared Poverty (Marxist) Method

While many people would be surprised at the "Marxist" label, this method is used most commonly. It is the method that most couples automatically expect to use after marriage. The concept comes from the old Marxist maxim, "From each according to his ability, to each according to his need." Both partners contribute any and all income to a common pool, and both take out of the common pool as their needs dictate. The simplicity, however, often ends here. Many times, as you might expect, the common pool does not cover both partners' "needs" or probably more accurately, their "desires." The result may be guilt, anger, depression, or even open warfare.

Because this method is used by so many couples, the shortcomings should be mentioned. The method goes sour in the following instances:

1. when one or both partners begins to feel exploited by the other;
2. when a power issue is at play, such as one partner having to ask the other's permission for a small purchase or personal item;
3. when one partner feels guilt over buying personal items;
4. when there is a significant increase or decrease in income without an accompanying decision regarding the changes in spending or savings.

5. When one or both partners wants more control over the spending habits of the other.

As potentially unfair as this method may appear, some couples are able to make it work. Usually this happens after certain ground rules have been established and followed. These ground rules include a sound and detailed knowledge of budgeted income and fixed expenses; an accurate idea of weekly, monthly, and yearly discretionary income; and a plan for savings.

If the method is not working well for *both* partners, the necessary first step is to discuss the actual source of dissatisfaction. Usually this results in more closely defined spending patterns, or more rigid limits for individual expenditures. It also could result in reworking the household budget. If no solutions seem reasonable, the couple may want to use a different budgeting method on a trial basis and re-evaluate after a set period of time.

The 50-50 Split

Like the Shared Wealth/Shared Poverty Method, the 50-50 Split is conceptually simple. Both partners split expenses 50-50. For instance, if the house payment is $800 per month, it is split in two with each partner paying $400. The process is the same for other expenses such as car payments, outstanding loans, utilities, food, insurance, etc. Usually couples who use this system use it only for joint expenditures, with each individual purchasing his or her own clothing and personal items from individual funds.

The key difference between the 50-50 and Marxist methods is the great psychological advantage of the 50-50 method. By specifically earmarking expenses as joint or individual, each person is free to choose his or her own individual purchases. Scott, who uses the 50-50 Split, states, "It lets me enjoy my hobbies more because I don't feel guilty about taking the money away from my family. Conversely, I never even think about getting mad when my wife buys a lot of new clothes—because it's all her money."

The 50-50 Split works well for many couples. It is simple, clear-cut, and usually fair. However, certain circumstances may make it unfair or unworkable. My own situation is a case in point.

Influenced by the Women's Movement, I wanted everything absolutely equal when Bill and I were married in the early 1970s. That was fine with Bill, so we decided on a 50-50 split on house payments, all household expenses, recreational activities, and vacations. All personal items such as clothing were left up to each of us individually, to come out of our own personal discretionary income after the joint expenses were paid. When we agreed to the arrangement it seemed fair, and we were both pleased with it.

What we did not take into consideration, however, was the wide disparity between Bill's income and my own. Being a few years older, Bill was already a tenured professor at the university, while I was just getting my feet wet trying out teaching on a part-time basis. What we failed to realize was that our lifestyle was on a par with Bill's income level, not mine.

I soon noticed that my entire income was being used to pay off my end of the 50-50. In fact I had trouble even meeting those expenses, and I was getting behind. At the same time, I observed Bill paying his 50 percent easily, with plenty of disposable income left over for his hobbies and what I considered frivolous indulgences.

What did I do? I took the intelligent, rational approach: I got mad. I complained. I blamed Bill. Fortunately, being married to a psychologist has some benefits. Instead of reacting to my anger with anger, Bill suggested that we look at other methods of budgeting our joint incomes. We did just that and worked out another arrangement that was more appropriate to our situation.

Our experience demonstrated a major problem with the 50-50 Split. *It won't work if the two incomes are not on the same level, or if the couple is living beyond the means of the individual with the lesser income.* It is a good system, however, for couples who can agree on splitting the cost of certain joint expenditures, and whose incomes are close enough that a 50-50 split is equitable.

The Percentage Split Method

While this system may seem a bit more complicated, it may be more fair, and in the long run need less readjustment than the two methods already described. The couples I interviewed who use this system are by far the most enthusiastic. Many couples, I found, have changed to this method after becoming dissatisfied with other methods.

Like the 50-50 Split, the Percentage Split Method assumes that there will be both joint expenditures and individual, personal expenditures. The ratio, however, is different. The ratio can be set at whatever split is reasonable for the couple's particular situation, such as 60:40, 48:52, 71:29. Each partner pays his or her allotted percentage of joint expenditures, and the remaining income becomes the individual's personal discretionary fund. This method works particularly well for couples who have large variations in salaries or for couples where one person works part-time, and the other full-time.

Of primary importance in the Percentage Split Method is that the ratio be mutually satisfactory to both partners. Coming to this decision may be more difficult than simply using the 50-50 Split, but the negotiation effort may pay off in the long run. Once the system is in place, it rarely needs more than minor modifications.

When negotiating the ratio, take particular caution that the person bearing the greater burden of the joint expenditure does not feel exploited. The factors you should take into consideration when negotiating the ratio include: gross and take home pay of both partners, outstanding loans, savings, and unpaid services such as housework, childcare, house repairs, car and yard maintenance. There may be other unpaid activities that should be considered, particularly those contributing to the overall welfare of the family or the appreciation of real estate, or other income.

Meridel and Jerry have used this method for several years and are satisfied with it. They originally established their ratio based on the proportion of income which each of them brought to the household. From time to time they have adjusted the ratio to more accurately reflect their financial situation as one or the other has changed jobs.

Their record-keeping system is simple. They both keep separate lists of amounts which they spend. Each includes a one- or two-word description after the amount (e.g., $95 groceries; $25 dog food; $8 movies). At the end of each month they tally up the total expenses and balance out the amount according to their ratio. Meridel says she usually ends up paying Jerry some money at the end of each month, but she usually pays fewer of the large expenses such as mortgage, utilities, and taxes.

Bill and I also have used the Percentage Split Method for several years. One variation we have made is to change the ratio annually. We base the ratio on the amount of income we each brought in during the previous year. We arrive at these figures when preparing our income taxes for the previous year, so the calculation of the ratio is no extra burden. The ratio of our two incomes for that year then becomes the new ratio which we use for the current year.

You could argue that the figures which Bill and I use are out of date because we are using the percentage from the previous year's income. This is absolutely true. However, neither of us sees it as a problem; we both recognize that the adjustment is made the following year. Also, it varies only minimally from year to year. If either of us were troubled about using the previous year's income ratio, we could use an estimate of the current year and make adjustments during the last month of the year.

Whether you set up a permanent ratio or choose to change the ratio annually, you will need to work out a system for monitoring the expenses on a day-to-day basis. Most couples use a system similar to the one that Meridel and Jerry use. They simply keep a tally of the amount spent on joint purchases and total them at the end of the month. This helps to monitor the system in general, and provides a convenient checkpoint to correct any imbalance.

Bill and I wait until the end of the year to even things up. When we prepare the taxes, we total the joint expenditures each of us has made. If, for instance, it turns out that one of us has overspent (and conversely, the other has underspent) we make up the difference with the proportion of tax returns due to each of us.

While the advantages of the Percentage Split Method are numerous, there are some disadvantages: (1) It is a nuisance to jot down expenses as they accrue and to total them at the end of the month. (2) If not monitored on a monthly basis, you may overspend or underspend your percentage and have a whopping deficit to make up at the end of the year. (3) If your income changes dramatically from year to year, your spending habits may not be in line with your new financial situation.

The advantages of the method are: (1) It is fair to both partners. (2) It allows the partner with the lesser income to pull his or her own weight.

Also, the individual's discretionary fund becomes extremely important for psychological reasons. Under the Marxist system a person might hide part of the household funds each week for personal expenses (not an uncommon occurrence, I'm told). Even if undiscovered, this type of action necessarily diminishes the mutual trust in a relationship.

On the other hand, the Percentage Split Method may add humor or appreciation for the other person's idiosyncrasies. For example, five years ago Bill spent about a thousand dollars for a grandfather's clock kit. To date he has never taken it out of the box. My reaction is one of amusement; I love to tease him about it. My reaction, however, would be much different if it had been *my* money which he used for the unfinished clock.

The Percentage Split Method often is the choice of couples who have been "burned" by previous relationships where there was an inequitable financial arrangement. Don't underestimate the psychological importance of fairness! While keeping a monthly tally may be a chore, most couples using the system report that they are more than willing to take the time to do this in order to feel okay about the arrangement. A number of men, previously in traditional marriages with non-working wives, indicated that this has been a primary issue when starting a new relationship. Because in their previous marriages they felt that they were continually being drained financially, they want a very structured financial arrangement in the new relationship. The Percentage Split Method seems to work well for these individuals.

Individual or Joint

If you choose to use either the 50-50 Split Method or the Percentage Split Method, there are many items you need to clarify from the outset as individual or joint. These are outlined in Table 3.3.

After setting the ground rules and clarifying the issues it is a good idea to set a time at which you will re-evaluate the method. I have found that one year is a reasonable time frame. Other financial milestones could be used, e.g., when a certain loan is paid off, when the last child finishes college, or before investing a large sum of money.

Table 3.3

Individual or Joint?
Issues to Clarify When Using a 50-50 Split or Percentage Split

1. *Which purchases are joint and which are individual?* What about cars and car repairs? Life and health insurance?

2. *What new joint expenses likely will arise over the next two to five years?* A new house? New car? Children? What are the priorities for these items?

3. *Will unexpected expenses such as medical or dental costs be individual or joint?* What if one partner wants contact lenses when glasses would be less expensive?

4. *Will all the children's expenses be joint?* What about airfare to the grandparents? Who will save for college? Does she share the child support payments which go to his ex-wife?

5. *How will outstanding loans be handled?* Loans from his college education? A loan on her car?

6. *How will savings and investments be handled?* Will some be individual and some be joint?

7. *What about unexpected losses or windfalls?* Who pays the settlement in his lawsuit? Who gets the lottery winnings from the ticket she purchased?

At the point of re-evaluating the system, you should consider its overall effectiveness including, of course, your emotional reaction to the method. Did one or the other feel cheated or exploited? Did many unexpected items come up that had to be negotiated on an item-by-item basis? What changes in your financial situation do you expect in the upcoming year? Would you prefer to try another method just for a change? What personal modifications would you make to this system to make it more to your liking? The bottom line is that both partners feel good about the arrangement, and not feel exploited or unduly burdened by the other person.

If you are both happy with your present system, and it does not portend future financial crisis for either partner, it is best to continue with the system that works and focus your energy on other areas.

Record-Keeping and Taxes

After working out a budget and choosing a personal shared budgeting method, you must make a clear-cut decision as to who will have the responsibility for the nitty-gritty work of paying the bills, keeping the records, filing the receipts, and preparing the income tax forms. Don't belittle the role. It is essential that complete, accurate records be kept, particularly when you are preparing taxes and when you are considering investments. It is my opinion that both partners should trade off the role so that both thoroughly understand the record-keeping system and can quickly retrieve information from the files.

If you plan to itemize your taxes, be sure that both of you know which type of records and receipts to retain. Over and over again I have heard couples arguing about the "stupidity" of the one who threw out some important receipts or records, or kept the records in such a disorganized manner as to be virtually unusable. To help with this I have included Table 3.4, the Tax Record Checklist.

For more specific information on income taxes, you may want to look at J.K. Lasser's *Your Income Tax*[1] which provides detailed information regarding deductible and non-deductible items. The initial section of the book is a valuable introduction to tax fundamentals and the remainder serves as a reference for more specific situations.

The person who takes on the role of record-keeper or tax-preparer should get proper credit for the time and work involved. Some couples treat the task as a household chore and factor that in when negotiating the household chores. If that's not in your arrangement, I would suggest at least that this person be given dinner out, a dozen roses, or a gift of his or her choice, perhaps annually after the tax forms are completed.

Discretionary Income and Major Purchases

Use of discretionary or disposable income (income after all the fixed costs have been paid) is probably the most sensitive financial issue. In many relationships there is a "spender" and a "saver." Or there is one who would choose a nicer home, while the other would choose a luxury vacation. Or one person wants a housekeeper, and the other prefers a sports car. The potential for differences goes on and on, but the point is that both individuals need to recognize their priorities and communicate how strongly they feel about each priority to one another. Then and only then can you make win-win decisions.

Table 3.4

Tax Record Checklist

Keep accurate and organized records and receipts for:

Salaries, wages, expense allowances, sick and vacation pay, severance pay, tips, bonuses, cash awards, back pay, jury fees, unemployment payments, and disability payments.

Other income such as interest, dividends, annuity payments, trust and estate income, alimony, rental income, pension income, insurance proceeds.

Medical expenses including physicians and clinic fees, medicine, crutches, wheelchairs, glasses, dental care, vitamins.

Home energy conservation and insulation expenses.

House purchase and/or sale including the price and terms, commissions, legal fees, capital gains or loss.

Business-related expenses including transportation, moving, business entertainment and gifts, professional association dues, union dues, uniforms, and work clothes.

Education including tuition, travel, books, and supplies.

Charitable donations and political campaign contributions.

Losses from theft or casualty.

All investment transactions.

Local and state taxes.

Childcare expenses.

Books, journals, and newsletters related to employment.

Home office expenses.

When making decisions involving a substantial amount of money, it is wise to consider the emotional impact of the purchase. For instance, my friend Phil always wanted a pool table. For him a pool table had long symbolized a lifestyle which he was attempting to attain—one of games and leisure. Understanding the psychological importance of this to Phil, his wife Barbara went along with the purchase, even though she had no desire for a pool table. There was barely room for it in their small basement recreation room, and it was difficult to squeeze around it to play a game. Nevertheless, Phil was fulfilling a fantasy which was more meaningful than the cost or inconvenience.

After a period of time, Phil's emotional attachment to the pool table subsided, and he willingly agreed to sell it. Barbara's tolerance for such a purchase has to be admired. Despite some expense and inconvenience, she let her husband pursue his fantasy, understanding its importance to him.

Other situations may involve substantially more money, and the trade-offs would weigh much more heavily than the cost of a pool table. In Table 3.5 one couple weighs the factors in the purchase of a sports car. Again, it is an emotionally-laden issue involving the husband's dream conflicting with the reality of college, vacation, and retirement savings.

Table 3.5
One Couple's Decision Regarding a Sports Car

Mary's List	Bob's List
1. We don't need an expensive sports car.	1. I've always wanted a sports car. It has been a dream since childhood.
2. We need to save the money for: a. children's education b. nice vacation next summer c. investment for retirement	2. The car has an excellent performance and repair record.
3. I would feel like we've cheated the children and me if we buy this car.	3. Over the long run the car will appreciate and have a good resale value.

The Discussion: Mary and Bob came to the negotiation session with these prepared lists of concerns. Because both agreed that they currently had the money to purchase the car, the discussion focused heavily on psychological considerations. After a lengthy conversation regarding current investments and savings for the children's college funds, they agreed not to purchase the car. Instead, Bob would save from his personal fund to purchase the car. If his other personal purchases were prudent, he would be able to purchase the car in about two years.

The timing of major purchases may be difficult even if there is no disagreement on the purchase itself. Some couples decide at the beginning of each year what purchases they would like to make over the course of the year; others wait until income taxes are prepared. Bob and Chris have a rule of thumb that they will make one major purchase each season. They jointly decide on a purchase and make their second choice the priority for the following season. Then as the new season approaches, they re-evaluate their prior decision. This way each major purchase gets dual consideration and the few months an item is "on hold" either strengthens or weakens their commitment to it.

A report card matrix can be a useful tool when you disagree over a major purchase. The example in Table 3.6 is that of a couple having difficulty deciding between a replacement television set for their old black-and-white one or an inexpensive microwave oven. Luxury items such as these usually pose the most difficulty for decision making. Couples rarely disagree on necessity appliances such as refrigerators or stoves, except perhaps on the brand or certain features. In this example, the process of rating the appliances and commenting on the various criteria helped them get a clearer perspective on the advantages of each item, and, especially, each other's point of view.

Table 3.6
Deciding Between a Microwave Oven or a Color Television

	Microwave Oven He	She	Television He	She	Comments
Cost	—	—	—	—	Not rated; cost about the same
Need	B	A	A	A	Both agree their old TV won't last long. She feels they need the oven to save time and energy.
Amount of Use Expected	B	A	A	A	Again, she thinks the oven will be used frequently. They both know the television will be used.
Psychological Satisfaction	B	A	A	A	Since she does more cooking, she rates the oven higher than he. They both would love a color TV.

After a long discussion this couple decided on the color television, with the microwave oven to be their next major purchase. They both indicated that rating the items was useful insofar as it forced them to comment on *why* they chose each rating. This opened up the discussion considerably.

Once the decision is made to make a major purchase, the choice still can be agonizing with the endless variety from which to choose. Many couples work out a deal where one of them does the ground work—gathers information pertaining to the product, checks the ratings in magazines such as *Consumer Reports*, and does the initial checking and pricing of the product, narrowing the choice down to two or three options. Then, going over the information with the other, the two decide on the final selection. This method has the advantage of saving time for the person not involved in the initial investigation, and the other can take pride in being the "expert" on that product.

Personal Financial Planning

Good psychological health is very much dependent on financial stability. If you're spending your time worrying about money, considerable time and energy is lost that could be put to use in other more creative endeavors. Financial planning, however, is very different from worrying about money.

Financial planning involves setting goals for yourself and following through with those goals. It includes looking down the road at where you want to be and the sacrifices you will make along the way. It takes into consideration taxes, retirement, and investments—low risk to speculative. Also, anyone working on a serious financial plan will, at one time or another, utilize the advice of qualified experts. Experts, however, are no substitute for clear thinking and analysis by both partners.

Savings and Investments

Probably one of the best things a couple can do to solidify a relationship is to work out a financial plan together. It is important that they both understand the plan and view it as a common goal. That way earlier "sacrifices" can be viewed as later payoffs. Also, joint decisions regarding the relative risks of any particular venture are likely to be better thought out than any single decision.

Considerations which will color the decisions you make regarding your financial plan will include: both of your ages, ages of any children, your tax position, your retirement needs, and your insurance needs.

Gerald Appel in *Double Your Money Every Three Years* has an excellent system of rating various types of investments by *return, risk, liquidity,* and *taxes.*[2] Depending on your particular situation, you may add other criteria for ranking various investments. Table 3.7, Rate Your Investment Chart, may be useful as a decision-making tool for both individual and joint investments.

Life Insurance

Life insurance gets a lot of bad press. The truth of the matter, however, is that if you have dependents, whether a spouse or children or parents, you need coverage. Venita VanCaspel has an excellent chapter on the topic in *The Power of Money Dynamics.*[3] She defines the various types of insurance including the best types of policies given for different personal situations. She also describes from whom to buy insurance—no small matter.

When making a decision on insurance, it is important that you both be informed and understand the types of coverage available. If you both do your homework and carefully weigh your own situation, you are less likely to regret your decision later. You may want to use one of the decision methods in chapter 1 to establish your criteria and evaluate the various policies under consideration.

Table 3.7

Rate Your Investments

Type of Investment	Return	Risk	Liquidity	Taxes	Level of Expertise Needed	Level of Monitoring Required	Other
Real Estate							
Money Market Funds							
Stock Market Funds							
Convertible Bonds							
Stocks							
Stock Options							
Corporate Bonds							
Municipal Bonds							
Commodities							
Collectibles							
C.D.'s, T. Bills							
Keoghs, I.R.A.'s							

A = Most Favorable   B = Favorable

C = Less Favorable   D = Least Favorable

Wills

Psychologically you may want to avoid the subject of wills. However, any legal or financial advisor will tell you that it is in your best interest (and your family's) to have one. Sylvia Porter lists the following reasons for writing a will in her *Money Book:*

1. To dispose of your belongings to those whom *you* wish in the proportions that *you* choose.
2. To provide for your loved ones in the best possible way.
3. To let all interested relatives and/or friends know your wishes.
4. To make it easier for your heirs to obtain and use what you left and to avoid fights and irritations.
5. To reveal aspects of your financial affairs that may be unknown to anyone else. (The very act of working up a will helps to disclose loose ends that need to be tied up.)
6. To ease the task of whoever is going to take care of minor children and influence the choice of any guardian.
7. To save many expenses.[4]

Also, if you as a couple have children or own joint property, it will make sense to have your attorney draw up both of your wills at the same time. Issues such as guardianship of minor children need to be clearly defined in both of your wills and not contradictory.

Because of the potentially complex legal nature of wills, I suggest you use an experienced attorney. Besides the issue of guardianship, you will want to consider the person you name as executor, provisions for the type of funeral or burial you desire, in addition to your wishes regarding the disposal of your assets.

Consulting Experts

Given current economic conditions, the average citizen is being forced into becoming money wise. Go into any bookstore today, and you'll find innumerable books on personal financial planning, and many other titles to guide you on your way to making a fortune. With this plethora of financial advice, how does one sort and choose, particularly with so many contradictory approaches?

Like any difficult question, this one has no easy answer. However, any good decision will be based on solid information seasoned with some common sense. Read some books, take some courses, and talk to others who are financially successful. The Recommended Reading section at the end of this chapter offers some excellent resource materials.

At some point, however, you will find that you need to consult an expert for critical, difficult decisions regarding your personal finances. Typically, the "experts" you would consult include the following: attorney, accountant, real estate broker, insurance agent, stock broker, and financial planner. Sometimes these functions are combined. Our accountant, for example, is also an attorney.

When you are investigating such experts, look beyond their fee structure in making your choice. Consider the nature and length of their professional experience, the type of client base they serve (are their needs similar to yours?), their performance record, and references regarding their integrity.

After you have consulted such an expert, weigh carefully the advice to see if it rings true. If it is highly technical, you might seek out another opinion. Look also to other people's experience for guidance. Talk to others who have faced choices similar to yours. What route did they take? Were they satisfied? If they had it to do over again, would they do it differently?

Once you have collected the data and received the information from the experts, the decision still may not be clear-cut. At that point I would suggest going over a best and worst case scenario to aid you with the decision. Then, making the decision jointly may decrease some of the fear inherent in a high-risk decision.

Recently Bill and I took a chance with an admittedly speculative oil investment. After thorough analysis, we decided that although it was high risk, the payoff was potentially very high. While considering the investment, we looked at the possible outcomes. The worst scenario would be that the entire investment could be lost. The best possible outcome would be that the payoff would be sufficiently high that both of us could reduce our current work commitments considerably.

However, in my mind the most critical element in the decision was that the money we invested was surplus. If, in the worst case scenario, all was lost, our lifestyle would not be changed significantly. The money lost could have been used to buy a new car or luxury vacation, but without it, our lives would go on as normal.

As luck would have it, the investment was lost. However, neither of us regrets the decision. We both still feel that if we had it to do over we would take the same risk. Because we made the decision jointly, neither of us is resentful toward the other for the loss. Recognizing that made the situation tolerable. Neither of us lost any sleep worrying about the investment, and for a few weeks we enjoyed many moments sharing fantasies about the good life we would have if our ship came in.

Recommended Reading

Appel, Gerald. *Double Your Money Every Three Years.* Brightwaters, New York: Windsor Books, 1974.

Hardy, C. Colburn. *Dun & Bradstreet's Guide to Your Investments 1984.* New York: Harper & Row, 1984.

J.K. Lasser's Your Income Tax. New York: Simon and Schuster, 1984.

Rolo, Charles J. *Gaining on the Market.* Boston: Little, Brown and Company, 1982.

Sylvia Porter's Money Book. New York: Avon Books, 1975.

VanCaspel, Venita. *The Power of Money Dynamics.* Reston, Virginia: Reston Publishing Company, 1983.

Footnotes

[1] *J.K. Lasser's Your Income Tax* (New York: Simon and Schuster, 1984).

[2] Gerald Appel, *Double Your Money Every Three Years* (New York: Windsor Books, 1974).

[3] Venita VanCaspel, *The Power of Money Dynamics* (Reston, Virginia: 1983), pp. 403–434.

[4] *Sylvia Porter's Money Book* (New York: Avon Books, 1975), p. 725.

4

Careers: Philadelphia vs. Phoenix—Who Gets to Go?

"If we could retire at age thirty-five instead of sixty-five, Bev and I wouldn't have any problems," states Dale, who works as an internal auditor for a large manufacturing company. Beverly, his wife, works as a manufacturer's rep in glass products. Both Dale and Beverly are on the road over 50 percent of the time. Frequently they don't see each other for four or five days straight. They both like their jobs, but want more time together.

In Chicago, Dennis and Arlene face a different situation. He wants to quit his job in marketing and start a consulting business on the West Coast where he already has several prospective clients. Arlene, who for the past five years has been developing a small restaurant, is now experiencing the success of operating a small business at a long-awaited profit. Both Arlene and Dennis feel justified in pursuing their career ambitions.

Nancy and Fred met and married while they were both in graduate school in Bloomington, Indiana. She was pursuing a master's degree in political science and he a doctorate in linguistics. Now, upon graduation, Fred has an opportunity to teach English as a second language in an elementary school program outside of Miami. Nancy has the possibility of two low-level research positions in Washington, D.C. Both prefer to teach at the college or university level, but the job market is closed in these areas.

Each of these couples faces very different, but serious career decisions. In none of the situations is the solution easy or clear-cut. In fact, the compromises and trade-offs available to each couple are fuzzy—subject to the whims of a fluctuating economy and a saturated labor market. What are they to do?

First, each couple needs to glean additional information to aid the decision-making process. Can Beverly and Dale obtain different positions which require less travel? Or can they work up to a level where they can set their own schedules and then coordinate them with each other? Can Dennis set up his consulting business in Chicago and allow Arlene to retain the restaurant? How long does Arlene want to keep the restaurant? If less than five years, would that be a better time for Dennis to relocate? Since none of Nancy's and Fred's job possibilities is really a first choice, what other career options do they have? In what geographic locations?

Career decisions are tough. Rarely do jobs turn out to be the "dream jobs" of your fantasies. Perhaps the salary is lower than you wanted, the demands greater, the travel more, or the assignment temporary. Multiply this by two careers and you've got a situation that seems impossible. But more and more couples face this situation daily.

Joint Career Planning

The most systematic approach to coordinating two careers is through joint planning. Each partner should put together an individual plan and then both should jointly review and consolidate them. Frequently people have trouble with the first step—determining an individual career plan. But once this first hurdle is overcome, joint career planning becomes easier and more feasible.

Individual Plans

Lifestyle considerations, such as those covered in chapter 2, are the first areas to be addressed in assessing your career situation. Basic questions like where and how you want to live necessarily determine your job and career choice. After that it's important to recognize what you want to get out of your work. Is security enough in itself? Or do you want recognition, risk, or adventure? Table 4.1, Work Values Clarification, is designed to help you work out your priorities and aid you in developing some career or job goals. It is a self-audit; there are no right or wrong answers. After completing it, compare your most highly ranked values with your current work situation. Which ones contribute to your work satisfaction? Does the lack of any of these values in your current job contribute to any dissatisfaction? These will be important considerations as you look at new jobs and career opportunities.

After determining what work values are most important, you will need to determine which career paths afford these opportunities. There is no need

---

Table 4.1

Work Values Clarification

Rank order the work values listed below. Don't be swayed by how you think you *should* rank them. Be honest with yourself and choose what is most important to you right now.

Creativity	Work which utilizes your talents or serves as an avenue of self-expression.
Independence	Setting goals and working at your own pace without directions from a supervisor.
Interest/ Knowledge	Work in a particular field of interest, using special skills or training.
Leadership	Decision making, planning and implementing projects, supervising others.
Recognition	Work which offers much visibility.
Rewards	Work which has a high monetary payoff or material gain.
Risk-Taking	Work which involves risks, is exciting and adventurous.
Security	Work which is comfortable, stable, and financially secure.
Social Service	Helping others in a positive way.
Variety	Work which frequently changes in content and setting.

Which of these values does your current job have to offer? Which are most important for your next position? Which ones are you willing to trade off?

---

to be in the dark about career options—resources are abundant. Since 1972 when Richard Bolles first published *What Color Is Your Parachute*, the bible of job hunters and career changers, a wealth of material on the subject has appeared. The Recommended Reading section at the end of this chapter offers several suggestions.

Career counselors and psychologists as well as various counseling centers offer a variety of vocational and aptitude testing services. These are tools which may be helpful in considering new career options. These tests do not determine the best job or career choice for you, but they can point you in the direction of careers that best suit you.

College counseling and placement centers have numerous resources for career changes; often they are available to the general public. Women's centers, Y organizations, civic groups, and even churches offer career workshops, seminars, and job fairs of various types. The librarian at your public library, too, may prove to be a valuable ally in directing you to reference materials on specific career fields, business directories, and career guidance materials.

The most accurate, up-to-date information you can get, however, will be that obtained directly from people who are already working in that field. "Information interviews" are brief conversations with such practitioners regarding the nature of their work, the appropriate education and experience for entering the field, and salary and promotion considerations. When setting up an information interview, make sure that you clarify that you are wanting information, not applying for a job, otherwise you may be referred to the personnel department.

Basic Information Interview Questions

1. What kinds of responsibilities do you have on your job?
2. How did you get your job? What education and experience is preferred for this kind of position?
3. What do you like and dislike about your job?
4. What future opportunities do you see in this field?
5. Who else do you recommend I talk to regarding careers in this field?

Most of the time you will get candid, honest feedback from an information interview. Be aware, however, that you are getting just one person's perception of employment in that particular field. Interview several practitioners in any given area before drawing any conclusions.

After assessing the information which you have accumulated from the various resources—books, counselors, work practitioners—you can put together a career plan. Plans involve setting goals and specifying actions to be completed by certain dates. Table 4.2 offers such an example.

Plans, of course, should be flexible and allow for serendipitous events. If your goal is to complete a master's degree in public health and start a professional position in that field in three years, then suddenly after two years you are offered an excellent position in public health, it would be foolish not to accept it and finish your master's degree at a slower pace. Or, if your partner is awarded a Fulbright to teach in Germany for a year, you might want to take a year off and go with him/her. Or, if as a result of some projects you have directed, you are offered a position in another company, you may want to revise your plan altogether if the offer is attractive and meshes with your long-range goals.

Table 4.2

Joleen's Career Plan

Overall Goal: To gain expertise in several areas of the human resource management field in order to become a qualified manager or outside consultant in four or five years.

Step One: Continue my position as a personnel representative doing employment interviewing. Talk to both managers and consultants to find out the most important areas in which to gain experience. Dates: Now until end of year.

Step Two: Rotate into labor relations, wage and salary administration, benefits, and/or training and development. Talk to more managers and consultants regarding opportunities. Dates: Over the next three years.

Step Three: Make decision whether to move into management or seek a position with a consulting firm. Talk to other professionals in the field. Dates: During the fourth year.

Step Four: Start new position as manager or consultant. Devise a new career plan. Dates: Fourth or fifth year.

Once you've established a plan, go over it with your partner. If your plan is to move from your present high-powered public accounting firm to a more relaxed position in industrial accounting in two years, how does that fit with your partner's plan? If you would like to go to law school in the evening, completing your degree in four years, how does that fit with your partner's plan? If you want to use your summer break from teaching to work in landscape design (with the idea that one day you'd start your own business), see how your partner reacts.

Much of planning is involved in anticipating problems and working them out in advance. If your partner knows that you plan to have a more relaxed accounting job in a couple of years, perhaps he'll be able to cut back somewhere in his position also, and you'll have more leisure time together. Or, if your partner knows you want to go to law school in the evenings, perhaps, she'll use that time to pursue an MBA. Or who knows, your partner might even be interested in landscape design—maybe he'll want to join you in the business.

Specific Job Offers—Whether to Take Them or Leave Them

After you have gone over your individual job plans with your partner and you set out to accomplish them, chances are you'll be faced with many decisions. Other careers may be enticing. Business associates may invite you to join them in new ventures. You may be offered a new position within your current company—or one with an outside firm.

In these situations you simply have to begin the evaluation process anew. Perhaps the new career alternative is more exciting or realistic or lucrative. Perhaps your associates have an offer that could catapult you to new horizons. Perhaps a new job would offer a fresh environment and more diversified experience.

For those contemplating a new job offer, be sure to evaluate where it would lead in terms of your current or revised plan. Is the position pointed in the direction you want? Will you get the necessary contacts and exposure? Will you enjoy the work and find it rewarding? Table 4.3, Criteria for Evaluating Job Offers, presents other considerations.

Table 4.3

Criteria for Evaluating Job Offers

1. Is the organization and its mission meaningful? Can you take pride in working there?
2. Is the work interesting and challenging? Is it meaningful?
3. Will you be able to use your creativity?
4. Is there enough diversity to be interesting?
5. Is there room for you to develop new skills and knowledge?
6. Will you gain visibility and professional exposure?
7. Is the work group friendly and cooperative?
8. Will the position likely lead to other advancements?
9. Is your office space pleasant and comfortable? Is it an environment in which you can be productive?
10. Is the location desirable?
11. Are there flexible hours and/or work sites?
12. How much vacation and personal time will you receive?
13. What other benefits (insurance, retirement, stock options, etc.) will you receive?
14. Is the salary offer attractive?

Geographic Moves

Certainly among the most agonizing decisions regarding jobs and careers is the question of a geographic move. "Relocation," the euphemism used by employers, is often one of the most stress-producing issues faced by couples today.

In bygone years relocation may have produced stress, but it wasn't questioned. Men accepted the moves required by certain companies and complacent wives followed. Non-working wives, or wives with "jobs" not "careers" were expected to go along wherever their husband's careers took them.

Not so today. With the trend toward dual-career marriages, both careers need to be considered whenever a geographic move is in question. And it's not always the women trailing the men. Seven to ten percent of all transferred employees are women[1]—a figure which will undoubtedly rise as women are promoted to prominent positions within the corporate world.

Also, there is a change in attitude of non-working women. More often than not, their role in the community, volunteer organizations, and their social network of friends are important considerations when contemplating a geographic move. Children, too, seem to carry more weight in such decisions than their counterparts of ten and twenty years ago. School and social involvement, athletics, and friendships all play a part in the decision today.

These added dimensions involved in making geographic moves have resulted in fewer automatic decisions to relocate. Employers are beginning to recognize the fact, acknowledging increased refusal rates. Current surveys on the topic indicate that one-third to one-half of employees asked to relocate are refusing. Ten years ago the refusal rate was less than 10 percent.

Table 4.4

Relocation Considerations

Availability of comparable or better position for partner

Opportunity for career advancement after relocation for both partners

Desirable community—meets your standards for climate and has amenities to fit your lifestyle

Housing market (includes ability to sell current house)

Cost of living change

Children's situation

Medical concerns

Social network

Educational concerns—school systems, educational institutions with graduate programs, retraining centers

Entertainment—theater, movies, restaurants, sports events

Proximity to places usually traveled—relatives, vacation spots

Change in financial status

Companies are beginning to look at these statistics and respond. With particularly valuable employees, both male and female, employers are taking actions to make the move attractive for both partners. Some companies will look for opportunities and outplacement for spouses. Other companies provide position referral for spouses within other companies.

While employer sensitivity to relocation is increasing and employer efforts to provide solutions to the accompanying problems are also increasing, this is still the exception, not the rule. For the most part, unless you have highly technical skills your company or your spouse's company may not have much to offer.

When considering a relocation, there are several factors to keep in mind. Table 4.4., Relocation Considerations, lists concerns pertinent to this decision.

Going Back to School

Because so many of the highly paid and well-respected jobs are ones which require years of education and/or highly technical training, it is not surprising that many adults are choosing to return to school. It is often a tough choice because the payoff may not be clear-cut or may be many years away. However, anyone who has suffered through a miserable, low-paying job, has at one time or another considered the option of going back to school—to finish high school, college, or pursue an advanced degree.

Many individuals add education to their long list of other commitments—job, family, community, and social activities. Others choose to trade-off and quit their jobs to pursue school, or cut down on outside activities to provide additional study time.

One factor aiding the person who chooses to go back to school is the wide variety of programs available in the public schools, community colleges, and universities. Many offer both full-time and part-time programs, frequently with a wide array of evening and weekend courses. Technical and vocational programs are offered at most community colleges year round. Even business and law degrees can be pursued on a part-time evening basis at many universities.

If the availability of educational programs is positive, other factors may not be as rosy. Tuition costs are high and increasing each year. Scholarships, loans, and other forms of financial aid may be an option depending on your situation and the school's level of funding.

Time may turn out to be a critical factor in the decision to return to school. There is always one more term paper, one more marketing project, one more speech, or one more computer program. No matter how much time you may have for studying, you always seem to need a little more.

Where will the extra time come from? How much will it affect your relationship? Will nine to midnight on Saturday night be the only time you have with your partner? How much out-of-class time do you plan to put into your courses? These decisions need to be faced directly by both partners.

Willingness to make sacrifices for your spouse's career is admirable, but only when the arrangement is reciprocal. Living in a university town, I have met several women who have fallen victim to the "medical student's wife syndrome." After working for five or six years to put their husbands through medical school, these women find themselves divorced at the end of a long, hard haul. It is acutely painful when these women discuss the extreme sacrifices which they made only to find themselves five or six years later with no marketable skills, no savings, and no plan for the future.

If you do choose to make sacrifices so that one partner can go to school, be sure to clarify what those sacrifices are and for how long they will last. Also, it is important to define your relationship after your partner has finished school. Will there be any change in the finances, division of household chores, or general lifestyle? Table 4.5 lists considerations for returning to school.

Table 4.5

Considerations for Returning to School

1. How does your educational goal contribute to your career goal? What kind of job market are you likely to face when you finish your degree? Will the courses enrich your current work? Is your degree likely to be helpful in reaching career goals five, ten, and twenty years from now?

2. How will the degree affect your earning potential? How much income will you lose (if any) by going to school?

3. How will it affect your lifestyle? What sacrifices will you and your partner need to make? What amenities will you enjoy after you have finished?

4. How long will it take you to finish?

5. How will you find time for study? How does your partner feel about this?

6. Will the tuition be an individual or shared expense? How much will it cost?

7. Does your partner have the same opportunity to go to school now? Or at a later date?

8. Do you plan to quit your job? Cut down your hours? Continue your current job?

9. What does your partner stand to gain?

10. What kind of emotional support will you expect from your partner? What kind will s/he be able to give?

Tough Decisions in an Unfair World

Given the reality of today's labor market, couples in which both partners are serious about their careers will likely face situations requiring compromises and trade-offs. Perhaps you will need to refuse a transfer in the interest of your partner's career. Perhaps you will need to make some financial sacrifices if your partner goes back to school. Perhaps you will have to take over more household and childcare responsibilities while your partner adjusts to a new position. The same holds for your partner.

When negotiating these difficult decisions, it is important to ensure that there is a balance of power in your relationship—that your partner and you share both the sacrifices and the gains. This is often difficult because in so many male-female relationships the man is a few years older and is further up the career ladder than his female partner. When it comes time for him to "sacrifice," the sacrifice appears greater because of his increased status.

Similarly, with women earning only sixty-two cents to a man's dollar, it is easy to decide to sacrifice the lower-paying position—which is usually the woman's. This kind of thinking can have detrimental effects on a relationship. Not only is it unfair, but it also affirms the sexist notion that men are more important than women.

So while it might be foolish for a man to give up an opportunity to make $80,000 at an executive level position so his wife can maintain her low-paid part-time job, it might not be foolish at all for a man making $30,000 to sacrifice a little so his female partner can move up in her career. This opportunity might mean that she too could reach and surpass that salary level.

The issue, of course, goes deeper than money. It touches on the type of relationship you want. If you respect one another and take the attitude that both partners should be happy and have successful careers, then career compromises and trade-offs will be necessary. If you both look upon career satisfaction as part of a positive life experience, then it will be necessary to set up a relationship where you can both experience those successes.

Supporting Your Partner
Through the Rough Times

No matter how much planning you put into a career there are always some unexpected twists. Your company may be bought out and you may find yourself unemployed. You may find yourself under a new boss who decides to make your life miserable. You may suffer from a long-term illness and be forced to give up your job. You may flounder in your newly established business that has eaten up your life's savings.

At these times your partner's support is crucial. When your career seems to be crumbling, you need your partner most—to boost your morale and get you moving on to more positive life changes. A sympathetic ear, a loving touch, and a warm embrace can make the difference between a normal upset and a protracted depression. If you can help your partner to re-establish confidence and realistic goals, you can re-establish your world. And you can probably make it a little better while you're doing it.

Recommended Reading

Bolles, Richard Nelson. *What Color Is Your Parachute?* Berkeley, Calif.: Ten Speed Press, 1984.

Figler, Howard. *The Complete Job Search Handbook.* New York: Holt, Rinehart and Winston, 1979.

Gates, Anita. *21 Steps to a Better Job.* New York: Monarch Press, 1983.

Kisiel, Marie. *Design for Change: A Guide to New Careers.* New York: New Viewpoints/Vision Books, 1980.

Kline, Linda and Lloyd L. Feinstein. *Career Changing: The Worry Free Guide.* Boston: Little Brown and Company, 1982.

Weinstein, Bob. *How to Get a Job in Hard Times.* New York: Simon and Schuster, Inc. 1984.

What to Do With the Rest of Your Life. Staff of Catalyst. New York: Simon and Schuster, Inc., 1980.

Footnotes

[1]According to Arlene Johnson, Program Manager, Catalyst Inc., New York. This figure is based on various data including the 1983 Merrill Lynch Relocation Management Annual Survey.

5

Children:
If, When, and How Many?

Deciding to have a baby is an emotional decision. It certainly isn't logical. If you were to look at only the logical factors—the cost, the time, the energy, the nuisance, you would have no difficulty in reaching a decision. And that decision would be a resounding no.

But because the decision to have children does involve emotional components, many couples have great difficulty with it. If they decide not to have children, they may have lingering doubts that they have missed an important life event. If they decide to have children, they may feel stuck with an irrevocable lifelong commitment.

For those who make the decision to have children the subsequent choices seem endless. How many children shall we have and how far apart shall we space them? Shall we have them in our twenties? Thirties? Forties? Other couples face even more complex choices concerning adoption, stepchildren, and starting a second family.

Also, the choices extend to lifestyle and parenting techniques. With the increasing number of working mothers and single parents, a full-time housebound mother is no longer the norm. Instead, a whole range of childcare and childrearing options is available. You need only to decide. But what an excruciatingly tough decision.

Logical Considerations

While the decision to have a child is in large part an emotional one, it would be sheer foolishness not to consider the logical components. Factors such as finances, career constraints, emotional and social readiness are critical.

Finances—The $300,000 Question

Children cost money. Over the long run they're a lot more expensive than fur coats and European vacations. Some economists estimate that one child will cost one-quarter of the family's income. In a recent article in *Money* magazine, Carrie Tuhy estimates that a couple with a current joint income of $50,000 will spend $278,399 to raise a son to the age of eighteen. A daughter will cost $17,000 more.[1] These estimates are based on the direct costs of food, housing, clothing, transportation, medical fees, and daycare. They don't include any salary lost by a parent who drops out of the work force, even for a brief period. Nor do they include the price of the added housework— around 19,000 extra hours over the eighteen years.[2]

Of course, there is a sliding scale effect with each additional child. By sharing clothes, toys, bedrooms, trips, and so on, there is a reduction with each child. Current estimates are that the cost of five children would amount to a little less than three times the cost of one child.[3]

Most of the expenses of raising children, however, come in the later years when parents are more capable of providing for them. College is the greatest single expense. Patricia O'Toole estimates that the total college costs for a child currently three years old will be $56,700 at a public university or $94,500 at a private school.[4]

While the amount needed to raise children does sound staggering, there are many ways to cut corners and save for college. Many parents concerned about saving for the children's education suggest investments which avoid high taxes such as Crown loans and Clifford trusts. Other parents become experts at finding garage sale bargains, taking low-cost camping vacations, and the like.

Children and Your Career

If money is a major consideration when deciding to have children, so is your career. It would be naive to believe that having a child does not affect your career. Its effect, however, may range from slight to monumental. You may find yourself in conflict with the two roles—that of provider and that of the loving parent who wants to spend much time with the children. It's not easy to explain to a three-year-old that you have to go to work when she wants you to to stay home and play Hungry Hippo with her. Or to a twelve-year-old that you can't make his soccer game because you have a sales meeting at the same time.

However, having a child need not ruin a career nor does having a career mean that you will need to sacrifice your role as a parent. People cope with juggling multiple roles every day. The majority of women are choosing to continue with their jobs and careers during the childbearing years. Chapter 8, Working Couples, provides useful information on managing several roles.

Until recently employers did not recognize dual-career marriages. It was assumed that every worker had a housewife to take care of things at home. With the large influx of women to the workplace, organizations are slowly beginning to change in areas significant to parents—allowing flex-time, recognizing the need for childcare leaves, and establishing on-site daycare centers, to name a few. Of course, some organizations are far ahead of others with these kinds of innovations. You will have to assess your own organization for practices which aid working parents, and factor this in with your decision to remain with your current employer if you do decide to have children.

To assess how much having a child would affect your career, check with some of your colleagues who have chosen to have children and note their reactions. What kind of problems, if any, does having children present? How do they cope? What do they trade off? What kind of support systems do they have? How many children do they have? What do they have to say about the timing and spacing of children?

Also consider the possibility of making the smoothest transition if you choose to have a child. Is summer a slow period at work? Might that be an optimal time to have a child? (Fate isn't always on your side with this kind of planning, but I have known several couples who conceived the exact month that they had chosen.) Consult your physician regarding fertility factors if you are in this situation.

After determining how having a child would affect each of your careers individually, it is important to share information with each other. Is it better that your partner receive her C.P.A. certificate before having the baby? Do you want to be promoted to district manager before having the baby? Do you both expect your lives to slow down in two years? These will be important points to discuss—they are questions which deal with *when* as well as *whether* to start a family.

Is Your Relationship Ready for a Baby?

Often couples who are fighting frequently or are having difficulty in their relationship will choose to buy a house or have a baby—in the expectation that the big event will make things better. If you are in this situation—choose the house, not the baby. It may cost you thousands of dollars, but it doesn't stay with you for the rest of your life. Having a child will not solve your problems, it will only create more.

Emotional readiness may be the single most important factor in the decision to have a child. Does each of you have the maturity to cope with all the changes which will occur? Can you envision the following: Yourself as a parent? Your partner as a parent? Solving child-related problems together? The day-to-day activities of infancy, toddler years, pre-school and grade school, adolescense, and finally having a grown child? Also, can you fantasize your partner and you handling a crisis together—picking up your child from school because of a behavior problem or making a trip to the hospital emergency room?

Don't panic. You needn't have a perfect relationship in order to make childraising successful. But it is important that you are on firm ground. If you have concerns about raising adolescents (and just about everyone does), you will have time to prepare. There will be resources—books, workshops, parenting classes, and professional counselors—available to aid you. What is important now is to feel positive about your relationship with your partner and to desire to have a child with that person. If you have a child, you will need to interact with your partner for at least eighteen years whether you have a good relationship or not.

Are You Socially Ready?

Having a child radically changes your lifestyle. It means loss of spontaneity and an endless need for babysitters. It means no more late Friday afternoon happy hours or leisurely Sunday mornings in bed reading the *New York Times*. A baby will drastically change your personal habits, the way you entertain, and the time you spend with your friends.

Are you ready for these changes? You may already have friends with children who have filled you in on their experiences. If not, do any of your friends anticipate having children? How do you currently spend your time with friends? How will having a child alter this? If the demands of a child force you to cut down on the time with friends, will you be resentful?

Both you and your partner should discuss your current social activities. What relationships would likely change after you had a child? What ones would likely remain the same? What new relationships might be established? Are you comfortable with the changes that you would have to make?

What scenarios can you imagine in which the presence of children would be a positive addition, e.g., trips to the zoo, decorating the Christmas tree, birthday parties? What ones are negative, e.g., missing a real estate class in order to attend a piano recital? Deciding to coach your son's baseball team rather than playing on your own team? Having to leave a party at midnight in order to get the babysitter home? How would you handle these situations?

Why People Have Children

To discuss why people have children may be like talking about the magnificence of the Grand Canyon or the beauty of Michelangelo's *David*—it borders on the ineffable. To attempt to put into words such intense feelings may be an impossible task.

In counseling couples who are deciding whether to have children this emerges as a difficult issue. The logical reasons *not* to have a child are clearly articulated: money, time, career impediments, lack of freedom. However, developing the opposing list is not so easy. Emotions are difficult to express; they also make you vulnerable to criticism. For example, to say "I want to have a baby because I love children" is a perfectly legitimate emotional expression. But it is open to attack from many angles. So is the comment, "I want to experience the closeness, love, and intimacy of raising a child." Somehow we allow the level-headed rationalist more power than the emotional romantic.

At the risk of sounding sentimental, I offer the following emotional reasons to have a child:

1. To develop a bond, a closeness that can only be established through the extensive interaction of a parent-child relationship.
2. To experience the intense joy of parenting.
3. To provide love, growth, and direction for a child who is part of your family.
4. To observe and participate in the emotional, intellectual, and physical development of your own child.
5. To expose your child to the riches and bounty of the earth; to enjoy sharing that bounty with your child.
6. To demonstrate the fun of play and set examples for sharing playful experiences.
7. To share your values and instill respect for others.
8. To give and receive affection.
9. To teach, show, and delight the child.
10. To enjoy each other's company.

Wrong Reasons to Have a Child

In coming up with appropriate reasons for having children, several inappropriate reasons also emerge. Unfortunately, we hear them with some frequency.

1. It will improve our relationship. No way.
2. Our parents want to be grandparents. Let your parents play with their friends' grandchildren—whom they've heard so much about anyway.
3. We want one of the other sex. Perhaps if you adopt, but otherwise you're taking your chances.
4. So I can quit my job and stay home. There are much simpler ways to accomplish this.
5. To carry on the family name. You may have only daughters who choose to take their mother's name.
6. Because our friends are having children. Will your friends also raise yours?
7. To have someone to take care of us when we're old. There's certainly no guarantee here.
8. To have someone who will give me lots of love and affection You'll be giving out lots and lots before you can ever expect to receive any.

Rockabye Maybe—Making the Decision

So you've looked at all the logical factors and have considered all the emotional ones. You've talked with your partner. They only answer that emerges is maybe. What next?

Next, check to see if the two of you share the same or different concerns about parenting. Are you both leaning in the same direction—either for or against having a child? Why or why not? Are you in agreement about wanting a child, but not sure when? Are you in agreement you don't want a child, but are concerned that you'll one day have regrets?

As in other negotiations, find your common ground. Discuss your areas of agreement thoroughly. Discuss the areas of disagreement thoroughly. Sleep on it. Consult a professional counselor.

Choosing Non-Parenthood

Until recently couples were expected to get married, stay married, and have their 2.5 children, no matter what. Today we are fortunate in having moved away from these restrictive norms. Not having children is a real option for couples, and large numbers are choosing this path.

Children are not for everyone. Sometimes it makes sense to choose non-parenthood for emotional reasons. Or for a fast-paced career. Or because you already have children in your life. Or simply because you don't want any. Many couples who enjoy children find the constraints of raising children in a nuclear family too demanding. They may choose to include children in their lives—but not their own. Frequently they will seek out relationships with children of friends, neighbors, relatives, or as a stepparent.

Just as deciding to have a child is an important responsible decision, so is the choice not to have one. However, just because this choice is socially accepted in the world at large doesn't mean that your individual families and circle of friends won't impose their standards on you. If you choose not to have children, it is important that you and your partner support each other at the critical times when family and friends pressure you about the decision.

You may also find yourself questioning your decision—perhaps as friends and colleagues start their families. Of course, you can always reconsider. But keep in mind that you are the best judge of what is best for you. Only you can make that choice.

Choosing Parenthood

You've made the decision whether, the next question is when. To be absolutely honest, there's not a perfect time to have a baby. In fact, there might not even be a good time to have one. Having a baby is never convenient. It's disruptive and impinges on many areas of your life. You will find yourself sacrificing leisure; you'll probably feel tired a good portion of the time. Everything will seem out of place. You may have second thoughts about your decision. Nevertheless, as with any important commitment, the long-term satisfaction and pleasure you receive more than likely will outweigh any short-term inconvenience.

Growing Up with Your Kids: Childbearing in Your Twenties

From a purely physiological standpoint the early twenties may be the best age for childbearing. At this time of life there is least risk to the mother and baby. The odds are in greater favor of having a healthy, normal child given the proper prenatal care, nutrition, and other health factors.

The psychological factors, however, may not be so favorable. Having children early in life places a major responsibility on the parents. It may be burdensome. Unless both parents are unusually mature, they may resent the baby which ties them down and forces them into a lifestyle requiring a steady income and innumerable chores.

Also, choosing to have a child at this point in life may force you to relinquish your own needs in favor of the baby's. For people not yet established in their careers, a baby can be demoralizing. A baby may be an obstacle to going to college, changing jobs, working, or enjoying a carefree lifestyle of travel and leisure.

Men are likely to react to a new baby with concern about being placed in the breadwinner role. This may mean seeing oneself stuck in a monotonous, limited job. It may mean feeling obligated to save for the baby's future when money is too tight even for current expenses. It may mean feeling that you have to give up career aspirations to take care of the very real needs of the baby.

Some women will react with similar concerns about finances and careers. Many, however, may feel pressure to become a housewife and primary caretaker of the child. It's important not to succumb to this pressure. Both men and women need to realize that children need not hold them back. It may take a lot of planning and sacrifice of personal time to combine raising a family with developing a career, but many young men and women are doing just that.

The positive side of early parenting is that you grow up with the kids, having lots of energy to work and play with them. You also have plenty of leisure at a reasonably young age after the children have left the nest. States Carol, "Now that all three children have left home, Jack and I are free to travel and pursue many hobbies that weren't possible when the kids were home. It's like a new-found freedom. Many of our friends with small children are envious."

The New Wave—Childbearing in Your Thirties and Early Forties

Delayed childbirth it's called. It's happening more and more. The children of the baby boom have chosen to start their families after they've turned thirty and after they've become established in their careers. They also have more material trappings to provide the children. The nursery may be custom decorated and the dressers filled with designer clothes in baby sizes.

While these "older" parents may still seem unusual, there are solid reasons for delaying childbirth.

1. *You can enjoy your youth without the hassles and responsibilities of early parenthood.* For those who come from the Me Generation of the Sixties, anything less than carefree college days feels like deprivation. Having experienced the freedom of the Sixties, the emphasis on self-discovery of the Seventies, these people now feel ready for the responsibilities of the Eighties and Nineties.

2. *It's easier to interrupt or modify an established career than a job in its initial stages.* Once you've reached a position of responsibility and authority it is easier to make adjustments. It's easier to plan how a child fits into your life, and it's easier to plan your work around the

changes in your personal life. Perhaps most important, you have more control over your own schedule—flexibility which greatly eases the difficulty of fitting children into a hectic life.

3. *Both partners have had an opportunity to mature and assimilate new values and understand the options for various lifestyles.* For most people it's easier to see choices after having had some years away from their parents. Those who choose to marry and have children right out of high school or college have little time to assess themselves. Many in this situation take on the values and lifestyles of their parents and raise their children as they themselves had been raised. For those in their thirties the choices seem more obvious. Perhaps for no other reason than having lived a few more years and collected more life experiences, these older parents tend to see many more choices of parenting than simply the style in which they themselves were parented.

4. *Money is not such an overriding, all-consuming issue.* Most people in their thirties and forties have established themselves at a level of economic security. There's little fear of unemployment, living from payday to payday, and making ends meet. Diaper service, daycare centers, tricycles, and bicycles are not luxuries. Older parents feel much less encumbered by children than their younger counterparts who find their children keeping them away from more fun-filled leisure activities.

5. *There's more opportunity for shared parenting.* Many couples who have waited until their thirties and forties to have children are two-paycheck couples who value the father's role in parenting on an equal basis with the mother's. This allows for an easier load for both parents.

Delaying childbirth is not without its problems, however. The following were noted by people who delayed childbirth until after age thirty.

1. *Increased concern over risk issues.* While ultrasound, amniocentesis, and other modern health techniques allow for greater detection of problems and abnormalities, there still remains concern over the well-being of the child. Thirty-five is the age most doctors ascribe the beginning of advanced maternal age. However, research has shown that factors such as inherited tendencies, previous health problems, and general physical condition are more important than age alone. Also, remember that when you read statistics for a certain age group, they include women in disadvantaged groups, who may not have

had the advantage of good diet, exercise, and proper prenatal care. Another factor to consider is that if you are willing to have amniocentesis and are willing to abort a defective fetus, you reduce your chances of giving birth to an abnormal baby to the same risk level of a woman in her twenties.[5]

2. *Increased concern over fertility.* Fertility decreases with age while the incidence of miscarriage increases. Consult your physician for an assessment of your individual situation.

3. *Concern over their own ages when the children reach school age.* This is much less a concern now when so many parents are having children in their late thirties and forties. However, some couples are worried that they will reach old age before the children have grown up.

4. *Concern about lack of energy.* Will we have the stamina to raise two children after age thirty? is a common question. While there are key contributing factors to this such as aerobic exercise, proper nutrition, good sleeping habits, it is still a concern to many potential parents over thirty.

Blended Families

It's easy to talk about Mom and Dad, the two kids, and Spot, but this family scenario is just not realistic for many couples. Blended families—families which are composed of children from more than one marriage, are as much a reality as the traditional one just mentioned. This modern day mélange brings with it complex issues—often very trying for both children and adults.

Parenting children you have raised since birth is difficult; imagine the difficulty of becoming a stepparent to children who have had different role models and methods of parenting. The potential for frustration, needless to say, is very high.

Take my colleague Janet. When she remarried she brought her three children to the marriage. Her new husband, Dan, brought his three children with him. In addition to Janet and Dan building their relationship, they also had to serve as counselors for the nine new relationships among the children (three new siblings per child). Janet says it took about a year for everything to smooth out into good working order, and I suspect this is faster than many families are able to manage.

Stepparents face a difficult role. They must not overstep their bounds and yet they must provide the love, discipline, and structure that they feel are appropriate for family life. They have to deal with the anger and hostility of children who may not have wanted their parents to separate. They may also face jealousy from children who wanted to remain the primary focus in their parents' lives.

The complex issues involved in stepparenting and in blended families call for clear communication by all involved. If anything, step-families force their members to be accepting of different role models and lifestyles. Compromise is often necessary. Your negotiation skills will truly be tested in this situation.

Starting a Second Family

Your kids are teenagers, or off to college, or just leaving home to strike off on their own. You're in a new relationship and life is flowing smoothly. Bang! Your partner brings up the topic of having children together. You may have briefly mentioned the subject a few times in the past. But this is for real. Time is running out for both of you. If you want to start a second family, you must begin now.

Since at least one of you has had children in the past, you'll be able to draw on some of the experiences to help you with the decision. Or will you? Perhaps not. If your first family was raised in a traditional male-provider female-caretaker situation, and now you have an egalitarian relationship, your experiences may not be relevant. Circumstances may be different the second time around. You may be more relaxed. Now there may be more conveniences—disposable bottles and diapers, snuglies, and jolly jumpers. So how do you decide?

Amanda and John based their decision on Amanda's desire to have a child. She states, "I didn't want to suffer the consequences of John's previous marriage in which he had two children." She made it clear from the start that she wanted a child with John. When they married John was aware of that commitment. Because of financial reasons, however, they chose to have only one child.

Doreen and Hal, on the other hand, decided not to have any more children, even though Doreen hadn't had any in her first marriage. Hal had two college-aged daughters living out of state. Their reasons were partly financial, but mainly based on lifestyle. They were comfortable in their current jobs and leisure activities. They chose not to interrupt that pattern.

Some areas to consider if you are thinking about starting a second family include:

1. Desire of both partners. Do one or both of you see having a child together as an important life goal? Can you feel fulfilled without a child? How do you think you will feel ten or twenty years from now if you choose to have a child? If you choose not to?

2. What are your respective ages? What implications do you face because of age, e.g., health risks, parenting responsibilities?

3. Lifestyle. Can you adapt to the lifestyle necessary to rear young children? Do you want to retain your current lifestyle?

4. Will a second family enhance your life and your relationship? Why or why not?

When you discuss the issues in starting a second family, be sensitive to your partner's bottom line. Some individuals clearly want a child and the only room for negotiation is the number. Others may be less certain about it and willing to go in either direction. Find out your partner's desire and communicate fully all of the related issues.

Adoption

Odds are that if you're considering adoption you've already considered many of the issues discussed in this chapter. The adoption procedure is so comprehensive and lengthy that, in all likelihood, you will have come to grips with questions frequently passed over by natural parents.

Laws and procedures vary from state to state regarding adoption practices. You will need to find out what applies to the state in which you plan to adopt and to live. Different agencies also will have different procedures and may vary on the length of time necessary to receive a child.

Because of the scarcity of infants and non-handicapped children, you will need to address the question of whether you want to adopt an older child, or one who is handicapped, or from another country or racial group than your own. These questions can be very difficult.

In addition to the issues already raised for natural parents, you will also want to consider the following:

1. Can we be good parents to someone else's child, particularly in a time when confidentiality is no longer guaranteed?

2. When the child disappoints us, will we be able to deal with the situation as if we were natural parents?

3. What kind of child can we expect from adoption? What kind of child can we live with?

4. How can we pave the way for our current children (if any)?

Because of the complexity of the laws and agency policies, it is necessary to obtain the best legal counsel available when undertaking an adoption. For preliminary information on adoption procedures in your area, check with your local public library for a listing of agencies and pertinent information. Consult other parents who have adopted children and talk to social workers in more than one agency.

How Many and When?

You may defer the question of how many until you've had your first child— the wait-and-see-how-it-goes method. Some couples, however, know at the outset they want only one child, or two, or three, or more. Since research has dispelled the myth of the problems associated with the only child, more and more couples are choosing to have just one. For some people it's easier to raise only one child. There are fewer schedules to deal with, the financial pressure isn't as great, and there is more time to spend with the child.

Couples who choose two or more children indicate that it is important to them that the children have siblings, not only for companionship and play, but to define more clearly the parameters of the family. If there is more than one child, there are clear-cut boundaries between the parents and children. The children have allies and see themselves as a unit. So do the parents. There are, however, more logistical problems with after-school activities and parent-child individualized time.

When considering the timing and spacing, you may want to consider the following:

1. What was your own family structure? What was your partner's? What are the positive associations? Negative associations?
2. What do you think is best for you? What do you think is best for the child?
3. Can your current housing accommodate the number of children you prefer?
4. What is the ideal spacing? Do you want them close together? Spread apart by a few years?
5. If conception doesn't occur within the time period you have established, how will you deal with it?

For every family who thinks they had the "right" number of children with the "right" spacing, you'll find another family with a different but also "right" number. Talk to your circle of friends and acquaintances and get their opinions. Talk to your partner and get his or her opinion. Read some books and get divergent opinions. Then make your decision and enjoy the days, weeks, and years awaiting you.

Recommended Reading

Bing, Elizabeth and Libby Colman. *Having a Baby After 30.* New York: Bantam Books, 1980.

Fabe, Marilyn and Norma Wickler. *Up Against the Clock: Career Women Speak on the Choice to Have Children.* New York: Random House, 1979.

Faux, Marian. *Childless by Choice.* Garden City, New York: Anchor Press/Doubleday, 1984.

Kappelman, Murray M., M.D. and Paul R. Ackerman, Ph. D. *Parents After Thirty.* New York: Rawson, Wade Publishers, Inc., 1980.

Lasnik, Robert S. *A Parent's Guide to Adoption.* New York: Sterling Publishing Co., Inc., 1979.

Noble, June and William. *How to Live with Other People's Children.* New York: Hawthorn Books, 1977.

Ourselves and Our Children. The Boston Women's Health Book Collective. New York: Random House, 1978.

Peck, Ellen and William Granzig. *The Parent Test: How to Measure and Develop Your Talent for Parenthood.* New York: G.P. Putnam's Sons, 1978.

Whelan, Elizabeth M., Sc.D. *A Baby?...Maybe.* New York: The Bobbs-Merrill Company, Inc., 1975.

Footnotes

[1]Carrie Tuhy, "What Price Children?" *Money*, Vol. 12, No. 3, March, 1983, p. 77.

[2]"The Cost of Raising Kids Goes Up," *Detroit Free Press*, September 23, 1982, p. 8C.

[3]"Facing Up to the High Cost of Kids," *Changing Times*, April, 1983, Vol. 37, No. 4, p. 32.

[4]Patricia O'Toole, "Can You Afford College for Your Kids?" *Redbook*, March, 1984, p. 48.

[5]Richard Saltus, "The Medical Facts on Timing a Baby," *Redbook*, February, 1983, p. 130.

6

Household Chores: Who Cleans? Who Sets the Standards?

"On Strike—No More Housework." So read the picket sign carried by a midwestern housewife a couple of years ago. Fed up with the responsibility of all the household chores, this woman picketed her front sidewalk for several days until her family was willing to hear out her demands. While this woman's action was decidedly extreme, she did make a point. Managing a household is time-consuming, energy-draining, and often unrewarding. People are usually oblivious to mended clothes, paid bills, or clean children, but the neglect of these chores quickly raises eyebrows.

Very few people claim to enjoy housework. For those who do like it, the satisfaction is usually in the finished product—the shining bowl—not the process of scrubbing it out. It is, of course, an understatement to say that housework is a source of conflict between many couples. If you are having difficulty reaching a mutually satisfactory arrangement, you are not alone. Many couples indicate that deciding to buy a house or have a baby is easier than deciding who will do the ironing!

Whatever your situation—working couple or one partner working and one at home—the division of household chores is a difficult negotiation. It involves many unspoken values, sex role stereotypes, and differing expectations. For men and women who come from traditional homes where certain work is women's work or men's work, it is often difficult to break away from these patterns. Often the blame is laid on the men for refusing to carry their fair share, and frequently that is the case. However, many women find it difficult to give up the responsibility and continue to carry the burden of housework along with full-time jobs.

Similarly, non-working women are currently expecting their partners to participate more in household maintenance. Such "housewives" are no longer slaves to the broom, but often carry out lives as active as their working counterparts, with their focus on children, hobbies, or volunteer services. These women, too, need to recognize the possibility of shared household chores, with the male partners taking an active role.

Although in the minority, "househusbands" also frequently find their partners' expectations regarding household chores much different from their own. Standards of cleanliness, frequency of chores, and amount and type of supervision over the children are areas of disagreement that often need to be negotiated.

Men Are Doing More: Women Are Liking It Less

A recent survey by *Working Mother* magazine sheds some new light on the issue of shared housework.[1] Not surprisingly, the survey indicates that men today are doing more housework than they were five years ago. However, the survey also indicates that today's women are feeling much more anger and resentment toward men on the housework issue than their counterparts of five years past.

Why this change in attitude? Are women really becoming that demanding? No, the survey authors explain. It is because the housework which the men have chosen to take over is precisely the work which women like best. The women, then, are left with the dirtiest and least desirable chores.

In looking at the chores that men have taken over, it turns out that they are the jobs which are flexible, visible, and sociable. These are chores in which the time pressure is not great, and there is much room for praise and recognition. For example, in the past five years more men have taken over cooking and reading to the children, leaving the women with chores such as diapers, dishwashing, and bathroom cleaning. With this in mind it stands to reason that women are finding themselves dissatisfied with the new division of labor.

This is not to say that men should not be doing housework. The survey results, however, indicate that there are some inherent problems with the break from a traditional arrangement to one with shared chores. A clear warning emerges from the survey: when allocating chores, be sure that both partners have some chores that are satisfying, and that both assume responsibility for some of the other dirty-but-necessary chores.

Grateful Isn't Great

One very common mistake made by many working couples is to assume unthinkingly that the woman should have complete responsibility for managing the household. A recent study of American couples by Philip Blumstein, Ph.D. and Pepper Schwartz, Ph.D. at the University of Washington indicates that working wives bear almost complete responsibility for the housework. In fact, even in situations where the husband is unemployed and the wife has a forty-hour per week job, the husband does less housework than the working wife![2]

Blumstein and Schwartz also looked at couples where both parties espoused egalitarian views, including the sharing of housework. These are the so-called "modern couples" who say they are dividing the tasks equally. The survey results, however, indicate that their actual practices are very different from a fifty-fifty split. In their book *American Couples*, the authors write:

> While these men do more housework than those who are in favor of a traditional division of labor between the sexes, they are still way behind their wives. On the questionnaires, we asked people how many hours a week they spent on household chores, such as cooking, laundry, and grocery shopping. The results were striking. While husbands might say they should share responsibility, when they broke it down to time actually spent and chores actually done, the idea of shared responsibility turned out to be a myth.[3]

For the most part couples have a long way to go in terms of dividing housework. Given this situation, it is not surprising that housework has become one focal point of the Woman's Movement. "Out of the Kitchen Uppity Women" has become a feminist slogan because the vast majority of women do assume responsibility for domestic chores.

Another common situation is of women showering their male partners with gratitude when they "help out" with cleaning, meal preparation, or domestic errands. Men, however, tend not to thank their female counterparts for carrying the full burden of running the household. They expect it. This kind of thinking not only is out-dated, but ultimately may prove dangerous to a relationship. Only when a couple has made a conscious decision that one will work for pay and the other care for the house and children, can this arrangement work, and even then it is fragile.

When columnist Ellen Goodman published her now-famous essay "When Grateful Begins to Grate" in 1979, many women began to realize that they fit the profile of "The Grateful Wife." In her essay Ms. Goodman writes:

> The Grateful Wife began to wonder why she should say thank you when a father took care of his children and why she should say please when a husband took care of his house.
>
> She began to realize that being grateful meant being responsible. Being grateful meant assuming that you were in charge of children and laundry and running out of toilet paper. Being grateful meant having to ask. And ask. And ask.
>
> Her husband was not an oppressive or even thoughtless man. He was helpful. But helpful doesn't have to remember vacuum cleaner bags. And helpful doesn't keep track of early dismissal days. . . .
>
> The wife would like to take just half the details that clog her mind like grit in a pore, and hand them over to another manager. The wife would like someone who would be grateful when she volunteered to take *his* turn at the market, or *his* week at the laundry.
>
> The truth is that after all those years when she danced her part perfectly, she wants something else. She doesn't want a helpful husband. She wants one who will share. For that, she would be truly grateful.[4]

Betty recognized that for ten years she has been a "grateful wife." In addition to her full-time job, Betty completely runs the household. Her husband helps with the evening dishes. Betty's mother frequently comments to her, "Aren't you lucky to have such a wonderful husband who helps with the dishes." But Betty no longer considers herself lucky. What she would prefer is a husband who would share fifty-fifty with the management of the household. Betty is becoming more and more resentful of her husband to the point that it is damaging their relationship.

Mary Lou is in a similar situation. She recently stood in the background at her daughter's graduation party and overheard all the rave reviews her husband was getting for the delicious outdoor barbecue. While the guests were complimenting his steaks, Mary Lou remembered her frenzied week with menu planning, grocery shopping, housecleaning, and preparation of all the food—except the steaks. She had taken on all these responsibilities on top of her full-time job and routine duties of transporting the children to swim meets, piano lessons, and softball games. She finally found herself at the party exhausted and resentful that her husband was receiving the praise.

What Betty and Mary Lou are facing is a fairly recent phenomenon—the return of women to the workplace without a subsequent change in responsibility for domestic chores. Perhaps because of sex role conditioning, women are not giving up old roles as they take on new ones. However, in many instances, the women would gladly give them up, but when no one is willing to take them on, they are stuck. What that leaves is the overworked "superwoman" who does not feel super at all. She feels tired. She feels overburdened. She has too many demands on her time. She needs to negotiate housework with her partner.

The Art of Love and Compromise

Cammie was also faced with the difficult role of taking on a full-time job without the subsequent sharing of chores by her husband, Mike. When Cammie talked to Mike about the problem, he was unwilling to change. He thought there was nothing in it for him. Not only was he still coming home every day to a clean house and home-cooked dinner, but he also benefited from Cammie's second income.

Cammie, however, being exhausted from the equivalent of two full-time jobs, was persistent in bringing up the problem. Mike felt she was nagging. It was not until Cammie was in tears and making threats of separation that Mike realized she was desperately serious. Then he agreed to take on some chores. At that point Mike indicated that he was willing to do more household tasks, and he really wanted to help out. However, he was afraid that his single friends would come around to the house and see him vacuuming. He told Cammie that he couldn't bear the humiliation.

While Cammie thought Mike's friends had a very unrealistic and macho set of expectations, she did consider Mike's feelings as critical in working out a compromise. Cammie and Mike came up with a division of labor that would not conflict with Mike's self-concept. Mike agreed to chores that embarrassed him least—running errands, grocery shopping, child care, laundry, and after-meal clean-up. Cammie agreed to continue cooking and other household tasks that included vacuuming, dusting, and mopping.

While this arrangement would not work for all couples—especially for women who think that Cammie's chores are the most odious, it did work for Cammie and Mike. In their win-win solution, she gained by having much of the overwhelming burden lifted from her. Mike also gained in that his willingness to take on extra responsibilities clearly indicated his respect and love for Cammie, and his desire to work out a better relationship. He also won in the sense that he would not be put in an embarrassing position in front of his friends.

There is also the possibility that as some of Mike's single friends get married and have children, their values will also change, and they too will be more accepting of men cooking meals and doing housework. At that point Cammie and Mike may renegotiate some of the chores and let Mike take over the vacuuming. For the time being, however, they have a solution which is acceptable to both of them.

What Men Have to Gain
from Sharing Household Chores

A man in a traditional marriage would probably think it ludicrous that he would have anything to gain by agreeing to clean out last night's meat loaf pan. If he has been in a relationship where both partners have accepted housework as the woman's responsibility, more than likely he will be reluctant to consider any change in the arrangement. And who in his right mind would give up time which could be spent reading, napping, or golfing in order to make peanut butter and jelly sandwiches for unappreciative third and fourth graders?

The problem lies in the changing world around us. We live a very different existence from that of our grandparents, where a clear division of labor between the sexes was not only desirable, but in many situations, a necessity. We have moved from primarily an agrarian to an industrial and now to a service economy. Corporate affirmative action programs are now aiding to eliminate the distinction between "men's work" and "women's work." And as more and more women move into the work force, they do not have time nor do they want the responsibility for managing a household.

But what about the old argument that many women willingly take on household chores and gain much satisfaction from it? That certainly is the case in some instances. I, for one, have enjoyed the pleasure of making bubbles with a laughing baby during bathtime. I have also felt a sense of accomplishment from making a chocolate mousse. I have even enjoyed the more mundane tasks of menu planning and grocery shopping. But men can and should be enjoying these special moments also.

What then do men have to gain by sharing the workload? The answer, of course, as it was with Cammie and Mike, is in the quality of the relationship and the potential for its development. Couples who share responsibilities and have mutual respect for one another face much better odds for a healthy relationship. If both partners can view themselves as a team sharing the chores, then there is much more potential for mutual understanding, respect, and accomplishment.

There is also a great danger in not sharing responsibilities. If one partner is feeling burdened by the housework or other activities, that person is going to become resentful. This may manifest itself in many ways. Typically one becomes too "tired" for sex. Or the over-worked partner may become nagging or a constant complainer. Or eat too much. Or get sick. However it manifests itself, it is bound to put a strain on the relationship.

A loving, caring relationship is simply not possible if one of the partners is feeling exploited. After all, a healthy relationship is based on mutual respect and a willingness to solve problems. Such relationships reflect a shared sense of responsibility for many facets of life—child-bearing, finances, career moves, and yes, especially housework.

Setting Standards

Remember the hilarious stage play and popular television show "The Odd Couple" with Felix, the fastidious roommate, and Oscar, the slob? While some of us have standards which approach those set by Felix, and others of us would be more inclined towards Oscar's brand of sloppiness, most people fall somewhere in between. However, even those of us who have "normal" standards for household cleanliness have a broad range of tolerance levels.

Bill, for instance, would not notice if the bathroom had not been cleaned in three months. Let someone take one small book from his bookcase, however, and he cannot rest until it is replaced and his books are in perfect alignment. Although I hate to admit it, I too have my own idiosyncrasies. As Bill has frequently pointed out to me, I put caps from bottles of ketchup and syrup sticky-side down on our white kitchen counters—and later forget to wipe up the spots. However, I cannot stand spills on the stove and have been known to wait with the sponge for the pot to boil over.

Everyone has a tolerance level, a dirt threshold, above which dirt, clutter, and messiness get on the nerves. This threshold is obviously different for different individuals, and varies from item to item and situation to situation. According to professional psychologists who have studied this phenomenon, people's tolerance for dirt also changes with their emotional state. When people are tired, hassled, or under stress at work, their tolerance levels usually fall. Conversely, when they are happy, their tolerance levels are higher.

Because of the variety and range of standards which are socially acceptable, and because of the potential for such a range even within an individual person, determining standards for two people can be exceedingly complex. Many couples find the solution by simply using the higher standard (whose ever it may be) so that neither person's nerves are shattered. In general this is a good, practical approach. In some cases it won't work, particularly if one person thinks many of the other person's standards are unreasonably high and too costly in time and energy. In these situations the couple will need to negotiate not only the chores, but also the standards.

Sarah and Tom found themselves negotiating the standard for their lawn maintenance when it got to the point that Tom was putting in over ten hours a week on the yard. He argued with Sarah that she should carry the bulk of the household chores since the yard demanded so much of his time. Sarah, however, countered that the lawn could be more than adequately maintained with one or two hours' work per week. She saw Tom putting in many hours needlessly on such activities as pulling up small weeds that he did not want in the ground cover. He also weeded, trimmed, and pruned every weekend— an activity Sarah thought unnecessary.

During the course of their negotiations, Tom began to realize that the yard work was psychologically very satisfying; he used it as a method of reducing tension and getting away from his office concerns. He wanted to continue putting in the time on the yard, even though he was willing to admit that it was not absolutely necessary. The result of their negotiations was that Tom agreed to continue doing the yard work, but to count only two hours a week as "household maintenance" time. He would continue to put in more hours on the lawn, but this would be considered "recreation" time for him.

Childhood experiences can color your reactions to chores and standards. Scott states, "It always bothered me as a child that my *mother* set the standards and *we children* did the work. Since most people like wonderfully maintained houses, yet few of us care for the drudgery of housework, it seems as if there's great potential for insensitivity and unrealistic expectations if one partner sets the standard and the other does the work." Scott's comments suggest that when both partners do housework, the standards become more realistic, balanced by the work required to maintain them. If especially high standards are expected by one partner, then the fair thing is for that partner to do the extra work.

Changing Standards

There are many instances in which personal dirt and clutter thresholds change. Often this comes after having children. Chris and Bob openly admit their standards have changed since they have had children. They are both marriage counselors themselves, and have consciously decided to give up some hours of cleaning for time together as a family. "One compromise we have made," states Chris, "is to keep the downstairs clean and in order—that is the area which our clients see. If there isn't time for a complete cleaning, we let the upstairs go." In their situation Chris and Bob have made a clear-cut choice, that family time is more important than clean bedrooms. As their children grow older they will probably go back to their former standards, but most important, they have worked out an arrangement which meets their needs for now.

Frequently couples also have difficulty in tolerating each other's methods of cleaning. Many women feel impatient or frustrated when their partners do not do chores exactly as they would. Often women have received very rigid training from their mothers and grandmothers as to how something should be cleaned, cooked, sewn, etc. It becomes ingrained at an early age that there is only one *right* way to do something. So, of course, it is irritating when a task is completed in another way.

My advice in this situation is to focus on the end product, not the process. If you are satisfied with the dinner, don't concern yourself that he pared the potatoes with a carrot peeler instead of a paring knife. If the dishes come out clean and sparkling, don't concern yourself that she washed them under the faucet instead of in the dishpan.

If you find that you still can't stand to watch him (or her) do the chore "improperly," then simply remove yourself from the situation. Chris says that she can't stand to watch how Bob does the laundry so instead of pushing her method on him, she stays away from the basement laundry area while he's doing the chores. Then when Bob comes up with the freshly laundered and folded laundry, she's happy, and there has been no criticism.

Short cuts are a different story. Both your partner and you likely will learn to share secrets for cutting down time spent on particular chores. Soon after our first child was born, I remember watching Bill making the baby's formula. The process was painstakingly slow. For each individual bottle he measured out powder and water, and then placed on nipples and caps. Then he would shake each bottle for a minute or two. I was able to show Bill how to cut down on over half the time by making a large batch in the blender and then simply pouring it into the bottle and capping it. Bill never went back to the old method—however, I was prepared to cope with watching him if he had insisted on doing it his own way.

You may also arrange with your partner to have certain areas which are your own domain, and where you do not impose standards on one another. I do not touch the clutter in Bill's study, nor does he tamper with mine. Similarly, in many relationships each person takes individual responsibility for his or her own car. Ralph refuses to drive his wife's car because it has so much junk in it. But instead of being critical, he simply uses his own. It is an arrangement that works out well for both of them. (And I suspect that he ignores the junk and borrows her car when his is in the shop being repaired.)

In the end you may need to negotiate certain standards. You may need to trade off some of your pet projects and you may need to compromise. If your partner thinks the children need a hot breakfast and you think Cheerios are just fine, you may end up with an arrangement where your partner fixes breakfast every day. Or you may work out an arrangement so the kids get a hot breakfast three or four days a week. Or you may end up with the kids eating Cheerios for breakfast daily, but having a hot lunch. All kinds of possibilities exist. Ultimately your creativity and sense of humor can help you learn to live with one another's idiosyncrasies—and who knows—you may even begin to enjoy them!

Four Methods of Chore Sharing

After interviewing numerous couples who have worked out satisfactory arrangements for sharing household chores, I have discovered that almost all the couples have gone through the following stages:

1. No formal delineation of chores. The person who had more time or noticed it, did it.
2. Period of dissatisfaction about the division of labor—frequently experienced by just one partner.
3. Serious discussion resulting in a rigidly defined division of chores.
4. Informal changes or formal renegotiation of chores as circumstances change.
5. Relaxation of some standards. Sharing of some chores. "Helping out" each other.

Not surprisingly, I found the key to such a process to be Step 3—undertaking a serious discussion and formal division of chores. Only when that was accomplished was there a point from which to trade or share or renegotiate. *A formal division of labor must be established as a starting point.* All the details should be worked out so that each partner knows whose responsibility is whose down to the last detail.

In order to get started in this process, I have included four methods for negotiating household chores. You may choose to use one or modify one to fit your own situation. When choosing a particular method, you will want to take into consideration your personality type as well as your partner's, your lifestyle, and other variables such as job and career constraints. For people who have no unusual circumstances, and who have never formalized their chores before, I would suggest the Negotiated List Method. The other methods may be useful depending on your particular circumstances.

Negotiated List Method

This is probably the most common method of splitting up household chores into an equitable arrangement. The first step is to draw up a master list of all chores you both agree need to be accomplished. Table 6.1, Checklist of Household Chores, may help you in enumerating the various tasks. You may have to add or eliminate some depending on your lifestyle.

Table 6.1

Checklist of Household Chores

Meals
  Grocery shopping
    Weekly
    Emergency
  Weekdays
    Breakfast
    Lunch
    Dinner
  Weekends
    Breakfast
    Lunch
    Dinner

Housecleaning
  By rooms:
    Kitchen
    Dining room
    Living room
    Den and/or family room
    Bathroom(s)
    Bedrooms
    Basement
    Hallways
    Garage
  By chores:
    Dusting
    Vacuuming
    Floor mopping
    Floor waxing
    Window washing
    Changing beds
    Wall scrubbing
    Cleaning counters &
      cupboards

Laundry
  His
  Hers
  Household
    Bed linen
    Towels
    Children
  Dry cleaning
  Ironing

Yard maintenance and house repairs
  Lawn mowing
  Garden, shrubs
  Spraying, trimming
  Snow removal
  Minor repairs
  Arrange for major repairs

Automobile maintenance
  Purchase gas
  Oil, tires, fluid checks
  Arrange for maintenance and repairs
  Insurance

Children
  Morning activities
  Evening activities
  Baths
  Help with school work
  Transportation
    to school or childcare
    after school
    evening activities
    weekend activities
  Arrange for childcare, babysitters
  Purchase clothing
  Special activities

Pets
  Regular maintenance
  Special care

Finances
  Keeping accounts and file systems
  Pay bills
  Insurance
  Investments
  Prepare tax forms

Other
  Parties
  Gifts
  Vacation arrangements
  Recreation arrangements

If there is disagreement on whether a particular task needs to be done, do not include it on the master list, but save it for later negotiation. You might disagree, for instance, that weekday lunches be on the list, if that is a sporadic chore. You also might choose to omit personal chores such as laundry, clothes shopping, or car repairs. In these cases both individuals would be responsible for their respective tasks.

Once you have a complete list, each person in turn chooses a task for which he or she has total responsibility and writes his or her name after the task. What happens, of course, is that each person begins by choosing the easiest, quickest, or most desirable chore. That's fine because your partner will probably find certain tasks much more desirable (or at least less distasteful) than you. As you near the end of the list, you may find that there are chores which both of you are reluctant to take. In this situation you might consider breaking down the chores into smaller components. Instead of "clean bedrooms" you could both choose to do one bedroom, or alternate, if there is an odd number of bedrooms. Similarly, you might break down childcare tasks by the child, so that one parent is responsible for one child's bath, and the other parent is responsible for the other child's bath.

If toward the end of the list you are faced with taking on a task that requires a skill you don't have (e.g., mending clothes, making house repairs, or preparing the income taxes), then you can (1) agree to do the task and learn the necessary skills, (2) throw out the task for the present and negotiate it later, or (3) hire someone else to do it.

After you have finished with this first list, take a look at your cumulative responsibilities and your partner's. Are they approximately equal in the length of time required to do them? Are they pretty much balanced in terms of desirability? Do your tasks conform to your current schedule or will you need to make changes? Do you anticipate any problems fulfilling your responsibilities? Do you expect your partner to have difficulty with this? Also, be sure to discuss the frequency and standards for particular chores that may have been problematic in the past. You may want to do some switching at this time. Or, if your lists appear imbalanced, you may need to do some two-for-one trades.

Next, you will need to take up any unassigned tasks which have been tossed aside. At this point the negotiations may get sticky. If there are tasks which one partner thinks are unnecessary or can be done with less frequency than the other expects, there will need to be some serious discussion. Can the person with the higher standards learn to compromise them? If not, in most cases it is best for that person to take on that particular chore, otherwise the partner with the lower standards is likely to feel resentful about taking on "unnecessary" work.

Also, if there is a task which both of you are reluctant to take on, could you hire someone else to do it? If you come to an impasse, you may want to utilize one of the other methods to resolve the issue, perhaps alternating responsibility for the chore, or giving extra credit for a particularly distasteful task. Table 6.2 illustrates a finalized negotiated list.

Table 6.2

Wanda and Joe's Negotiated List

Wanda's Chores	Joe's Chores
Groceries	Prepare formula and baby bottles
Children's laundry	Purchase food from health co-op
Wash large pots & pans	White wash (his and hers)
Children's baths	Launder socks (his and hers)
Children's haircuts	Launder towels and bed linens
Change diapers	Snow shoveling
Childcare arrangements	Garbage
Oven cleaning	Care of dogs
Polish furniture	Load and unload dishwasher
Entertainment arrangements	City driving
Vacation arrangements	Income tax preparation
Clean cupboards	Repairs

Shared Chores	Individual Chores
Meal preparation	Purchase own clothing
Children's morning and bedtime activities	Own laundry
	Gifts and greeting cards
Transportation to and from childcare	Own car maintenance
Lawn and yard work	
Parties	

Weekly Cleaning Person

Vacuuming
Dusting
Kitchen counters
Bathrooms
Walls
Change beds
Special projects as necessary

As a last step in the Negotiated List Method, post the list in a prominent position where you will both see it. A refrigerator door, cupboard, or bulletin board is a good place where you both can glance at it and make sure each of you is living up to the agreement. You also might agree on a date to re-evaluate the system and post the date on a joint calendar.

The Rotation Method

Unlike the Negotiated List Method, the Rotation Method offers flexibility to couples who can shift their portion of the workload to accommodate each other's schedule. It is a particularly good method for couples in which one or both partners works in highly seasonal industries such as retailing, public accounting, or construction.

In its most simple form couples rotate household responsibilities. This occurs usually on a weekly or monthly basis. Table 6.3 illustrates the method Sarah and Don use, where they simply alternate responsibility every other week. If one of them falls behind or doesn't do the chores, it remains that person's responsibility until it gets done.

Table 6.3

Sarah and Don's Rotation Method

Sarah and Don alternate every other week doing the following tasks:

> Vacuum apartment
>
> Dust living room
>
> Clean bathrooms and kitchen
>
> Buy groceries
>
> Laundry

Because they are both gone during the day, they only eat evening meals at home. Sarah prepares dinner on Mondays and Wednesdays and Don prepares dinner on Tuesdays and Thursdays. They leave weekends open for going out or entertaining.

Another variation of this method starts with a joint compilation of all household chores to be assigned to either partner. Instead of dividing the chores in an even balance, the couple allocates a heavier load to one partner for a given period of time. At the end of the time period the couple reverses the ratio so that the partner with the previously heavy workload gets the lighter amount.

This method works extremely well for Harold and Mary. Harold runs a painting business and Mary is an elementary school teacher. Harold's business is at its peak in the summer months when Mary is not teaching. From May through September Mary takes on the lion's share of household chores and childcare responsibilities. Then, during the winter months, when she is busiest, they reverse the chores and Harold takes over the burden. Table 6.4 illustrates the method they use.

Table 6.4
Mary and Harold's Rotation Method—by Seasons

SUMMER MONTHS

Mary's Chores	Harold's Chores
Grocery shopping	Children's baths and bedtime
All meal preparation	activities
All laundry	Lawn and yard work
Children's transportation	Minor repairs
Entertainment arrangements	
Almost all errands	
Car care	
Most unexpected chores and emergencies	

WINTER MONTHS

Mary's Chores	Harold's Chores
Grocery shopping	Weekday meals
Weekend meals	Car care
Some laundry	Children's baths and bedtime
Some errands, children's activities	activities
	Children's transportation
	Income tax preparation
	Majority of errands
	Christmas shopping
	Some laundry

YEAR ROUND

Weekly cleaning person does vacuuming, dusting, bathrooms
Children responsible for own bedroom, pets, help with meals and clean-up

---

Notice that in their version of this method they do not reverse roles completely. Mary enjoys cooking so she continues with that role on the weekends during the winter months. Similarly, Harold enjoys the bedtime activities with the children and continues doing that during the summer months unless he stays on a job beyond their bedtime.

On paper Harold and Mary's division of labor seems clear-cut and well-balanced. However, Mary notes that this isn't always the case. "The months of May, June, September, and October are incredibly busy times for both of us," she notes. "Often we have to work out the details on a day-to-day basis. However, the system does work well for us in the summer and dead of winter. Also, because my teaching schedule affords me more flexibility even during my busiest periods, I am able to pick up some of Harold's responsibilities if he gets tied up with his work."

Task-Sharing/Task-Splitting

On the surface this method seems idyllic. Picture a man and woman in their country kitchen slowly and blissfully preparing the evening meal together, while the children play quietly in the next room. Then they sip wine and cuddle in front of the fireplace while dinner cooks. It's all very romantic and, of course, completely unrealistic.

In most cases, couples don't arrive home at the same time to start fixing dinner. Furthermore, most couples do not have the time for elaborate meal preparation, nor are most children patient enough to wait an hour or two for dinner. Task-sharing may be a good idea, but it is not always practical. Time constraints, work schedules, and outside demands frequently prohibit this method from working. There are, however, a few situations where task-sharing can work.

Task-sharing can work in situations where both partners have compatible schedules and enjoy each other's companionship while doing chores. Many couples work out an *ad hoc* housecleaning session on Saturday morning. They have certain chores which need to be done, and they both work together until all are completed. Frequently couples with children share childcare chores, doing baths, storytime and bedtime activities together.

Other couples work out some task-splitting arrangements. Bill and I, for example, split up lawn mowing. He does the large open parts of the lawn with our huge, riding tractor mower. I, in turn, mow around the trees and side hill with the hand mower. The arrangement satisfies both of us, although occasionally our lawn is only partially mowed, depending on our respective schedules.

Task-sharing can be a workable arrangement if both partners have time and flexible schedules. However, for many couples it works out only for large projects such as moving or house painting or remodeling. Otherwise the method may be used for entertaining or an occasional meal.

Bonus Method

While the Bonus Method is a little more complicated than some of the other methods, it has definite value in equalizing chores that either require a fair amount of time or skill or are simply unpleasant. This method may appeal to couples who have not previously been satisfied with their division of labor—when both partners believe their arrangement is inequitable. It may also appeal to partners who have consistently done the "dirty work" and want credit for it.

The Bonus Method may seem extreme unless you've had difficulty negotiating certain chores. It is detailed and is meant for use with particularly troublesome chores, while you use another method for the more routine tasks. The Bonus Method works by crediting each partner points for completing certain tasks. Credit is given for the time necessary to complete the task along with bonus points for special skills required. It also includes a "dirt bonus" for such unpleasant chores as sick room clean-up and unclogging drains. Because the method is so involved you should consider it as a last resort. However, several couples indicated that they had success with this method when other methods simply weren't working.

Table 6.5

The Bonus Method

CAROL—Week of October 12

Task	Time (1 hour=10)		Dirt Bonus		Skill Bonus		Total
Mend Steve's clothes	10	+			10	=	20
Ream out drain	5	+	10			=	15
Change car oil	5	+	10			=	15
Vacuum house	10					=	10
				Carol's Weekly Total:			60

AL—Week of October 12

Task	Time (1 hour=10)		Dirt Bonus		Skill Bonus		Total
Rinse, soak, and wash diapers	10	+	10			=	20
Fix dishwasher	10	+			10	=	20
Clean bathroom	5	+	10			=	15
Laundry—wash, fold, put away	20					=	20
				Al's Weekly Total:			75

Table 6.5 illustrates this method. In this example, Carol and Al set a minimum of fifty points apiece which they each must acquire by the end of the week. They have not included grocery shopping, meal preparation, and a number of other routine chores which they have been able to share without disagreement. What they did choose to put on the list are tasks that neither wanted to do. At the end of the week Carol totaled sixty points, Al, seventy-five. Carol will carry over ten points into the next week; Al will carry over twenty-five—the amount they earned over fifty.

There are several psychological advantages to using the Bonus Method:

1. It equalizes chores by time, e.g., sewing on a button is not equated with making a child's Halloween costume.
2. It gives credit for tasks requiring a particular skill or certain level of expertise, and may encourage each partner to gain new skills.
3. It gives credit for those distasteful but necessary chores of day-to-day living.

Child Labor

Most couples with children suggest getting the children involved with the chores at an early age. Often it takes time and patience to train a young child to do the job properly, but the payoff is high later on. The child gains a sense of family responsibility and accomplishment and the parents are relieved of some time-consuming tasks. Clearing the table and picking up toys are chores that a child as young as two or three can do. When children reach school age, they can often take on more chores such as sorting and putting away laundry, watering plants, and feeding pets. When they are in late elementary school, they can vacuum, dust, mop, and do most heavy cleaning.

The irony, of course, is that the older the children become, the less they want to help out. My three-year-old, for example, would love to unload the dishwasher and put the dishes away—breaking a half-dozen dishes in the process. On the other hand, my six-year-old, who is much more capable of the task, is not at all interested in doing it, favoring a book, game, or television.

There are different ways to involve children's participation in the chores. The most common seems to be simply laying down the rules. Mom and Dad tell John to do ABC, and Jane to do XYZ. John and Jane know that Mom and Dad aren't joking so they do it. Other families allow the children more choice, letting them choose their favorite tasks. Other families switch chores from week to week or month to month so that tasks are rotated. Sometimes families use a point system where each member must earn a certain number of points weekly. Certain tasks hold certain point values, so that you can negotiate for the higher valued tasks to meet your quota.

Although some families prefer to keep allowances completely separate from household chores, they can be incorporated. Some parents pay children on a task basis; others pay the child a given amount weekly for a list of chores completed. Other parents designate particular chores as the child's responsibility and pay the child for any extra chores beyond the designated ones. Often older children are compensated for babysitting with younger brothers and sisters. Lawn-mowing, yard work, and a variety of housecleaning tasks are commonly assigned to young people.

For ideas on motivating and rewarding children to help with the chores consult *401 Ways to Get Your Kids to Work at Home* listed in the Recommended Reading section at the end of this chapter. This book offers methods which appeal to children such as charts with stars and other non-monetary rewards.

Hiring Help

Although it is an expense that not everyone can afford, hiring someone to do the household chores can save you much time and energy. Frequently couples choose to have someone come in to clean on a weekly or bi-weekly basis. The pool for such services is vast, from the teenager next door looking for extra money to the professional cleaning services listed in the yellow pages. Your budget, the type of cleaning you expect, and your particular lifestyle will influence your decision. Table 6.6 offers some ideas.

Table 6.6

Where to Find Household Help

Friends and Neighbors. Ask for their recommendations, particularly people they are currently using and have found reliable.

Community Newsletter and Bulletin Boards. Post your own ad and indicate times, tasks, and fees.

Local Colleges and High Schools. Inquire at the counseling office and financial aid and placement offices. There may be bulletin boards where you can also post a notice.

Newspaper Ads. Place an ad in your local newspaper. Prescreen over the telephone to establish type of arrangement, transportation, fees, etc.

Yellow Pages. Look under "House Cleaning." These services may be expensive and require minimum fees.

A weekly cleaning person who comes to your home and does the vacuuming, dusting, kitchen and bathroom cleaning is a common arrangement. Of course you can work out whatever arrangement you want. Sometimes the most convenient arrangement for couples with small children is a dual childcare and cleaning person. If you have babysitters coming to the house anyway, you might want to offer them more money for housecleaning and meal preparation.

If your budget is limited, you might want to consider a teenager who can come in and help you out with the cleaning. Usually you will need to train the person step by step in how you want the job done, but after the initial training period, very likely you will have positive results. One caution: young people often need a lot of supervision. It is best if you can work along with them, or at least be in the house to answer questions and supervise the process.

Also keep in mind that two people, if well supervised, can get the job done in half the time of one. After the birth of our second child, I was feeling overwhelmed by some very large cleaning projects—floor waxing, window washing, and oven cleaning. When I realized the fatigue of having a new baby was getting me down, I hired two college students to take over the large projects. To my surprise they had everything completed and were asking for more work in about four hours time! For a few dollars I was able to lift the burden of these extra projects off my shoulders and enjoy the new baby and a sparkling house for the rest of the summer.

When you make a contract with a cleaning person it is essential that all of the specifics be worked out in advance. I would advise that you have the applicants come over and look at your home, and that you go over a prepared list of chores.

Once you are satisfied that you have found someone who will work out, you will want to negotiate a fee. For teenagers working with you under your supervision, and where you have differing projects from time to time, I would suggest a per-hour fee. For a cleaning person coming into your home doing regular chores each week, I suggest a comprehensive weekly rate. You then avoid the issue of paying slow workers more than fast, energetic ones. In determining reasonable fees, check with friends and neighbors who have used cleaning people and find out the going rates in your community.

If you choose to hire someone who will come in and clean your house in your absence, you must find someone who is absolutely honest and reliable. I suggest that you check references before even setting up an interview. Find out how long they have been with others, why they left, and if there were any problems. Also check on such issues as food, transportation, and social security. If you go through an agency such as those listed in the yellow pages, check out in advance if you have to pay a finder's fee.

Deciding What Not to Do

Sometimes couples are able to save time by jointly deciding not to do certain items. That way they can both cut back on their respective chores. This, again, goes back to the question of standards, of how much dirt and clutter you both can tolerate, and how much you'd rather use the time to do something else. Neither Bill nor I care if our bed is made daily, so our bed goes unmade except for the one day a week our cleaning person comes in. We also take short-cuts on meals by frequently inviting Ronald McDonald and Colonel Sanders to dinner. Our Labrador retrievers are better than a broom for cleaning up the floor around the high chair after the baby has eaten.

Some couples have freed themselves from responsibilities by buying condominiums rather than houses. Others use public transportation rather than bother with the hassles of automobile ownership. Still others have switched from formal entertaining to potluck dinners. Table 6.7 offers some more activities that you could eliminate in the interest of time.

Table 6.7

Chores You May Decide to Eliminate

Making beds	Comforters can be pulled up over the bed, if the sight is a distraction.
Ironing	Always buy permanent press. Give away old clothes requiring ironing.
Formal meals	Perhaps sandwiches or scrambled eggs would taste just as good as a time-consuming formal family meal.
Entertaining	Have a potluck or go out to a restaurant. Hire a caterer if formal entertaining is necessary for business purposes.
Drying dishes	Let them dry in the drainer.
Dusting	Eliminate knick-knacks and dust collectors from every room.
Folding laundry	Put underwear, socks, etc. back into their respective drawers without folding. Sort them as you use them. Put towels back on the racks, and bed linen back on the bed without rotating.
Floor waxing, wall washing, carpet cleaning, window washing	Hire someone to come in once or twice a year and do it all at once.
Errands	Keep a grocery store list, department store list, and drug store list. Combine when possible. Wait to go until the list is long or the errand is absolutely necessary.

The Quality of Mercy

While the purpose of this chapter is to aid couples in negotiating household chores so that each partner has responsibility for a significant portion of the chores, I feel that it is necessary to add a bit about compassion, love, and growing relationships.

Because of life's cyclic nature, we rarely live on an even balance. Most of us have experienced high points clustering together, perhaps in the same day, week, or month. Similarly, the crises group themselves together, sometimes becoming so overwhelming that coping seems impossible. Sometimes the cycles are predictable. The Christmas season is a period of great difficulty for many people. Other troublesome times center around anniversaries—often of a parent's death or another traumatic event.

The pace of life changes. Going back to school, changing jobs, and starting a family are all events that create heavy demands on people. Such times can be very stressful. If your relationship is to survive you will have to weather the many ups and downs and changes in pace experienced both by your partner and yourself. Mutual support during the rough times is a critical element of a good relationship.

With that in mind, it makes sense to relax the rules now and then. You may choose to ignore an unmopped floor or unmade dinner until the crisis has passed. Or you may choose to help out by doing some of your partner's chores during the time that is particularly stressful. If you are confident in yourself and your negotiation skills, there is no danger that you will end up with all the chores. You can, after all, renegotiate them. For, in the end, if you want a warm, sharing, loving relationship, it is necessary to be warm, sharing, and loving.

Recommended Reading

Aslett, Don. *Is There Life After Housework?* Cincinnati, Ohio: Writer's Digest Books, 1981.

Cruse, Heloise. *Help! from Heloise.* New York: Arbor House, 1981.

Mayer, Gloria Gilbert. *2001 Hints for Working Mothers.* New York: Quill, 1983.

McCullough, Bonnie Runyan. *Bonnie's Household Organizer.* New York: St. Martin's Press, 1980.

McCullough, Bonnie Runyan and Susan Walker Monson. *401 Ways to Get Your Kids to Work at Home.* New York: St. Martin's Press, 1981.

Raintree, Diane. *The Household Book of Hints and Tips.* New York: Ballantine, 1979.

Winston, Stephanie. *Getting Organized.* New York: Warner Books, 1979.

Footnotes

[1]Laura Lein and Lydia O'Donnell, "Big Deal," *Working Mother* (February, 1983), pp. 71, 106–109.

[2]Phillip Blumstein, Ph.D. and Pepper Schwartz, Ph.D., *American Couples* (New York: William Morrow and Company, Inc., 1983), p. 145.

[3]Ibid., p. 145.

[4]Ellen Goodman, *At Large* (New York: Fawcett Crest, 1981), pp. 107–108.

7

Housewives & Househusbands: Balancing the Power

Dick and Leon paused to talk for a few minutes during a work break at a local childcare co-op. They were both putting in the required four hours per week to keep their three-year-olds enrolled in the co-op. Dick mentioned that he had several loads of laundry waiting for him at home. Leon responded that he also needed to do laundry, and he had no idea what he was going to make for dinner. Both agreed that the housework seemed endless and their wives "just didn't understand."

While this example may seem far-fetched, it's actually taking place across the country. New househusbands are taking over roles that previously belonged exclusively to women. Such role reversals are increasing because of economic necessity and personal choice. Dick made no decision about his new-found role; he was laid off from an auto plant eighteen months ago. Leon, on the other hand, recently quit his job in order to pursue a med-tech program at a local college. Both of their wives are working full-time to support their families.

America has recently begun to awaken to the fact that men can and do make good homemakers. In fact, movies such as *Kramer vs. Kramer* and *Mr. Mom* as well as television shows and comic strips are reflecting men in these new roles. While the media is having fun with this new image, the reality is that men are moving into traditionally female roles, and society is accepting it. It's no longer unusual to see men with children at grocery stores, laundromats, playgrounds, and dentists' offices. Fathers are accompanying their children on school trips and taking care of them when they're sick.

Many factors contribute to this. The increased divorce rate, along with the new popularity of joint custody, means more single fathers in custodial roles. Also, money pressures have pushed many wives into the workforce, leaving more men with household and childcare responsibilities. Other couples, particularly two-career couples, are choosing to divide the responsibility jointly. Then there are the new househusbands.

Even with their new visibility, however, the number of full-time househusbands is low. Although their numbers are increasing, men currently make up only a small percentage of the full-time homemakers in this country. According to U.S. census data, men who were out of the labor force because they were keeping house, increased from 81,000 in 1950, to 296,000 in 1971—an increase of 264 percent.[1] As their numbers continue to increase, these men are likely to change both the status and responsibilities of homemakers. The change will be welcome.

Until these changes take place, however, househusbands will stand as a vivid contrast to the thirty-five million women in this country who are housewives. Until househusbands become commonplace, the status of the housewife is likely to remain unaltered—regrettably low. This situation is particularly unfortunate because most housewives have an enormous workload as well as a responsibility of mammoth proportions—raising children from infancy into adulthood.

While lip service is given to the traditional housewife, extolling her self-sacrificing virtues, in fact, the housewife has been relegated to a position with little power, security, or status. Rae André, author of *Homemakers the Forgotten Workers,* states that housewives are victims of a "domestic double standard."[2] They are being told that they are serving a lofty goal and at the same time are being put in a situation that provides no monetary rewards, no prominence in the labor market, and no long-term security. In fact, even the word housewife carries a stigma. This time-honored profession is no longer viewed with respect.

The domestic double standard is at the core of the difficulty one encounters when choosing to stay home rather than to join the paid labor force. When one partner works for pay and the other doesn't, the uneven balance of power can create a myriad of problems.

If you or your partner chooses to stay home rather than work for pay, then you will need to be aware of all the underlying issues that accompany homemaking and be prepared to deal with them. It is not impossible to work out a mutually satisfactory arrangement with your partner. You will, however, need to be aware of the complexity of the issues and face them head-on as you begin your negotiations.

The Best of All Worlds; The Worst of All Worlds

Homemaking has much appeal. You are your own boss. You set your own hours. Your time is flexible. You have few deadlines. You can even take a nap in the middle of the day!

Perhaps more important, you have the opportunity to interact with your children for extended periods of time, and you can do much to create a warm, loving home atmosphere. In short, homemakers have a golden opportunity to positively influence family relationships.

But the reality of the housewife's lifestyle may be very different from this rosy picture. In fact, sociologist Jessie Bernard studied husbands and wives of traditional marriages twenty years ago and came to some startling conclusions. She found traditional housewives suffered from poor physical and mental health with ailments such as nervousness, insomnia, headaches, dizziness, and heart palpitations. She concluded that traditional marriage was healthy for men, but the "anachronistic lifestyle of the housewife" was making women sick and driving them crazy.[3]

While women may not be in the dire straits they were twenty years ago, housewives as a group have not significantly improved their lot. They still lack power, prestige, and security. They are expected to be nurturing, but not to be nurtured. They are on call twenty-four hours a day. Their labors frequently go unrecognized and unrewarded.

If Dr. Bernard's findings are an accurate portrayal of the housewife, then why have so many women left the paid labor force to become full-time homemakers in the first place? For many there has been no choice. The role is more or less imposed by family and society. A woman grows up with the idea that she will quit work when the first baby arrives, and unquestioningly she does.

For women who do make an active decision to stay home, the choice may be easy. Paid employment for many women means a monotonous job with low wages and rigid hours. The job of housewife at least allows for better working conditions with flexible hours and variety of tasks. It also has social approval, particularly when there's a baby or small children.

But these are only short-term gains. Giving up a low-status job often precludes a woman from working her way up to a better position with better work conditions. Frequently women stay out of the workforce for such a length of time that they become virtually unemployable. So if the long-range effects of housework turn into stress and depression, many women find themselves unable to go back to paid employment. They become trapped at home with uninteresting and unchallenging work. They also may deplore their own financial dependency on their partners.

So the housewife may find homemaking far better or far worse than paid employment. She may find homemaking pleasant earlier in life, but stressful and uninteresting later. Or she may find it pressured and demanding when the children are young, and lighter and more pleasant once they're in school.

As forward thinkers and as win-win negotiators we need to recognize both the positive and negative aspects of homemaking. We need to recognize that as a lifestyle it may be very attractive or very depressing. Most of all, we need to recognize it should be an option for both men and women.

Negotiating to Stay Home

A number of issues arise when you discuss the possibility of one partner staying at home. These include issues of time, money, work, and childcare. Facing these issues will help you set a positive tone for your relationship and help you avoid later problems. In your negotiations you may also want to consider options other than homemaking such as part-time work, home-based work, and special projects from outside employers.

When starting your discussion, be clear about your expectations. If you see your partner's workbreak as a six-month maternity leave in which caring for the baby and finding subsequent childcare are the only priorities, be sure and communicate that with her. She may feel an obligation to bake pies and hand-sew quilts. On the other hand, if you expect your partner to take over all the household chores, you'd better make that clear from the start.

An obvious first question that needs to be addressed is one of duration. How long do you expect to be out of the work force? Three months? One year? Until the kids are in kindergarten? Or college? Until you get your M.A.? Or finish your dissertation? If you are taking a leave from your work with a specific contract date, then you will be able to answer this question with precision. However, if you need to conduct a job search before going back to work, your time frame will be more ambiguous. Nevertheless, you should set a date with a few weeks or months leeway.

Next, you will need to negotiate a financial arrangement. Will your partner support you? Will you live off your own savings? Or both? For how long? The "Money and Power" section of this chapter as well as chapter 3, Personal Finances, should be helpful.

Then you will need to outline the responsibilities of the homemaker partner. What chores do you expect this person to handle? What are the standards of cleanliness? Chapter 6, Housework, should be useful in providing some guidelines.

If you will be taking care of children, you will also need to outline the related tasks and schedules, and discuss any standards—particularly those which have been problematic in the past. If you are staying at home with your first baby, you may not be aware of all the responsibilities, but you can anticipate some tasks such as laundry, diaper changes, feedings, and middle-of-the-night interruptions.

If your arrangement is long-term or indefinite, it will be essential to re-evaluate it from time to time, perhaps on an annual basis. You will want to ask yourself the following questions:

1. Are you both satisfied in your current roles?
2. Are either of you envious of your partner? In what ways?
3. Would part-time paid employment be better for either of you? What about full-time employment for both of you?
4. Would a complete role reversal be attractive to you?
5. Do you think that the stay-at-home partner is pulling his or her fair share?
6. Do you feel that the working partner is contributing enough to the relationship?
7. Is your financial system satisfactory to both of you? Are you both covered for the future with individual savings and pension plans as well as insurance?
8. What changes would you like to make?

In the end, if homemaking doesn't work out, it's important to give yourself or your partner the option to return to paid employment either part-time or full-time. Sometimes the fantasy just doesn't turn out to be the reality. Instead of lying on the sofa sipping a ginger ale and watching the Channel Five afternoon movie, you may find yourself with a colicky baby, ten loads of laundry and a broken-down washing machine, and a dog that's in heat.

Money and Power

Money determines power in many realms—business, government, politics, and in most homes. How you work out your finances will be a key determinant in the distribution of power in your relationship.

The old cliché is accurate—money talks. Money makes decisions. Recent research indicates that in traditional marriages the more important the decision, the more likely the male is to make it. In studies of marital decision making, researchers have found that men tend to make decisions regarding issues outside the home such as employment, money, friends, and housing. Non-employed wives make the lesser decisions regarding home decoration and food preparation.[4]

The financial arrangement a couple works out is critical in establishing a basis for future negotiations in other areas. Both partners must feel satisfied with the arrangement and both must feel free to renegotiate if the original arrangement doesn't work out. In too many traditional marriages, couples have failed to realize this and have built up mutual resentment. The wage earner becomes angry at the partner who never brings in any income, and the non-earning partner becomes so dependent on the wage earner that he or she cannot make critical decisions or speak out on important topics. This kind of arrangement is unhealthy and inhibits a win-win relationship.

The financial issues outlined in chapter 3 are essential and need to be spelled out when negotiating an arrangement where one person works and the other stays home. In addition to these issues you will also need to determine if the partner staying home will be paid for his or her responsibilities. If so, how much? At what intervals will this be evaluated? How will you measure whether both partners are keeping up their ends of the agreement?

Whatever arrangements you come up with, the non-earning partner should have a personal fund which is totally discretionary. Psychologically it is essential to be able to make personal purchases without first getting approval from the wage-earning partner, or—even more demeaning—having to ask him or her for the money. If the non-earning partner does not have a personal discretionary fund, then the balance of power is tipped almost totally to the wage-earning partner. This situation is a set-up for power plays and other destructive behavior. Imagine the guilt which some homemakers must feel when they hide a few dollars of the grocery money each week to save up for something personal—not an uncommon occurrence even today!

It is also important for the non-earning partner to have adequate savings and retirement plans. You need to be prepared for unpleasant contingencies. Divorce (which can come after fifty years of marriage) threatens many who are solely dependent on their spouses for support. The problems of displaced homemakers have come to national attention in recent years. These women have been left (by divorce, a spouse's death or desertion) with little or no economic support and few skills to compete in the job market. It is not a pleasant situation to face, although three million women currently fall into the category.[5]

If you are a homemaker, you can establish in Individual Retirement Account (IRA) in your own name. Similarly, it would be wise to set up other savings and investments to protect your future. Just as it's important to have your own personal fund now, it's equally or more important to insure your future.

Unpaid Drudgery—The Work That's Never Done

If in your agreement with your partner you take over traditional homemaking responsibilities, undoubtedly you will find that there are numerous tasks which are not only onerous, but never-ending. For some people it will be housecleaning chores such as vacuuming, dusting, or mopping. For others it will be related to childcare such as packing lunches or cleaning gerbil cages. Still others will object to tasks requiring long hours and extreme patience such as sewing or furniture repair.

Such thankless jobs can be difficult to tolerate, but you may need to accept them in exchange for the more positive elements of staying at home. Since the burden is on you, you will need to create your own reward system for accomplishing these chores. Perhaps you can try doing the worst first. If you do the unpleasant chores during the morning hours, you may be able to reward yourself with the afternoon off.

Another tactic is to seek recognition from others. Write a note on the kitchen blackboard, "Hurrah for Mom—she shampooed the carpets today," or "Because of Dad we all have clean sheets tonight." Or make a chart to post on the family bulletin board. Give yourself a gold star for each chore you accomplish. After twenty-five or fifty stars, buy yourself flowers. One caution: rewards are important, but stay away from food and liquor for this purpose. Neither you nor your partner would appreciate the consequences.

Round-the-Clock Interruptions

Being on call twenty-four hours a day may be the greatest pressure on a full-time homemaker. If a child starts crying in the middle of the night, it is usually the homemaker's duty to respond. If the plumber has indicated s/he will come sometime between 10:00 A.M. and 6:00 P.M., the homemaker must alter his or her schedule and stay home all day. If a neighbor calls and needs another parent to help with the elementary school's book fair, it's the homemaker who is expected to attend.

Jean, a former social worker and now a full-time homemaker, says, "It's the surprises in my day-to-day schedule that I find most bothersome. While some people might like a break from the routine, it irritates me to have to drive a forgotten lunch over to the school or to get a call from relatives I've been waiting for all morning, saying they won't be here until sometime in the afternoon. I guess these little things wouldn't bother me so much except my family always expects me to be available."

Jean's reaction is not isolated. Many of the homemakers I interviewed were annoyed by their partner's or family's attitude toward their own time. "It's not so much that I'm unwilling to do the task," states one homemaker, "but they seem to think that I'm here to take care of anything at a moment's notice. I resent it when my husband calls me and asks me to drop off his reading glasses at the office."

This homemaker makes an important distinction in the type of chores which she sees as appropriate and inappropriate. She currently is doing the latter chores, but not without resentment. It is these areas that she could usefully choose to negotiate.

When you negotiate to stay home, it may be useful to compare the homemaker's job with paid employment vis-à-vis coffee breaks, lunch breaks, and hours worked per day. Most paid workers on call twenty-four hours a day such as firefighters and doctors are compensated by extra money and more time off. Homemakers may need this rationale for claiming time for themselves and setting limits on what they should do. A workaholic executive has come to be frowned upon, but a workaholic homemaker is, unfortunately, still the norm.

Of course, the tables can turn. A working partner may come to be resentful about chores that aren't done well or simply aren't done by the stay-at-home partner. If this situation should arise, then you will want to discuss your standards and take a look at what is a reasonable workload for the stay-at-home partner, and set some minimum requirements.

Hints from Househusbands

Fifteen years ago I had never heard of the term househusband, much less met one in the flesh. Since then I have personally known and interviewed at least two dozen. After talking to men who have moved into homemaking roles, I find that many have a much different style and approach than women in similar roles. I believe that these men have some real insights to offer their female counterparts. The following are some general observations:

1. *Most men viewed their roles at home as temporary.* They expected to go back to work at some future point. Some even had dates in mind. Some saw themselves as being between jobs. In fact, most of these men did go back into the labor force within a few months or years.

2. *Most men did not take housework as seriously as their female partners.* As a group they tended to be serious about childcare, but few viewed the housework component of homemaking as a career in itself. They might view certain chores as necessary, but in the total scheme of things, unimportant.

3. *Most had outside interests which they pursued during the day.* Hobbies, sports, or reading are frequently cited as important to the structure of the day, often coming before housework or routine tasks.

4. *The men relaxed household standards once they realized the time-consuming nature of housework.* If Johnny didn't have a clean pair of socks for the following day, Dad might suggest wearing the same pair for two days. If there wasn't any food in the house for dinner, Dad might suggest eating out. If there was a ring in the bathtub, Dad might not even notice.

While I'm not advocating slovenliness, I do think that women can learn something from these new househusbands. And that is *balance*. It's important to balance work with play. It's important not to take yourself or the chores too seriously. Most importantly, give yourself the option to quit. If full-time homemaking doesn't work out, be prepared to discuss opportunities for part-time or full-time paid employment.

Negotiating to Go Back to Work

This is a tricky subject, particularly for women whose husbands believe that a woman's place is in the home. If this is your situation, you need to bring him up to date about current lifestyle choices. Perhaps he has already witnessed a number of women working in his occupational area. If this is the case, you may already have a sensitivity to his objections.

But focus on your own situation. What are his objections to your working? Perhaps they are problems that can be worked out with some creativity. If he is concerned you might not be able to fix breakfast in the morning, discuss it and examine some compromises or trade-offs. If he is concerned that you won't make enough to pay for a babysitter, take a look at the figures of your long-range earning capacity. Or perhaps he has some irrational concerns that you can dispel for him. When it comes right down to it, you need to convince him that he has much to gain (e.g., more sympathy, support, understanding, money, fun) by your working. Then the battle is won.

Written resources may be valuable to both of you. Start with the Recommended Reading at the end of this chapter. You may be particularly interested in *How to Go to Work When Your Husband Is Against It, Your Children Aren't Old Enough, and There's Nothing You Can Do Anyhow* by Felice N. Schwartz, Margaret H. Shifter, and Susan Gillotti.

Towards New Horizons

Labor forecasters predict a trend toward more flexible work practices in the paid labor force. This means that in the future we should be seeing more flex-time, part-time jobs, job-sharing, shorter work hours, increased vacation time, and childcare leave for both fathers and mothers. As these changes are realized, both men and women will find it easier to enter and leave the paid labor force. The sharp dichotomy between the full-time breadwinner and full-time homemaker will become blurred.

Discussing new roles for men in their book, *The Two-Career Couple*, Francine S. Hall and Douglas T. Hall write:

> ...men are cutting back on working hours, putting in less travel and overtime, and focusing on the quality of their lives rather than on the quantity of their earnings or success. They are also measuring success in new ways. They are doing more role sharing at home, in some cases, and they are getting more involved in their role as parents. This does not mean they are turning into women. They are simply claiming roles that they had a right to all along. Both sexes, then, are not really branching out into new roles as much as they are exploring *all of their own roles* for the first time.[6]

The choice of paid employment or homemaking *for both men and women* may in the end have a humanizing affect on us all.

Recommended Reading

Beer, William R. *Househusbands.* South Hadley, Mass.: Bergin and Garvey Publishers, Inc., 1983.

Friedan, Betty. *The Second Stage.* New York: Summit Books, 1981.

Levine, James A. *Who Will Raise the Children? New Options for Fathers (and Mothers).* Philadelphia: J.B. Lippincott Co., 1976.

Minton, Michael H. with Jean Libman Block. *What Is a Wife Worth?* New York: William Morrow and Co., 1983.

Schwartz, Felice N., Margaret H. Schifter and Susan S. Gillotti. *How to Go to Work When Your Husband Is Against It, Your Children Aren't Old Enough and There's Nothing You Can Do Anyhow.* New York: Simon and Schuster, 1972.

Footnotes

[1]William R. Beer, *Househusbands* (South Hadley, Mass.: Bergin and Garvey Publishers, Inc., 1983), p. 10.

[2]Rae André, *Homemakers The Forgotten Workers* (Chicago: The University of Chicago Press, 1981), pp. 9–27.

[3]Jessie Bernard, *The Future of Marriage* (New York: Bantam Books, 1972), p. 30.

[4]Sharon Price-Bonham, "Marital Decision Making: Congruence of Spouses' Responses," *Sociological Inquiry* 47 (1977), pp. 119–125.

[5]André, pp. 186–187.

[6]Francine S. Hall and Douglas T. Hall, *The Two-Career Couple* (Reading, Mass.: Addison-Wesley Publishing Co., 1979), p. 61.

8

Working Couples:
Double Problems or Pleasure?

The two-paycheck marriage may be the most important social change of the twentieth century. Sociologists are ranking the widespread entry of women into the work force as a major sociological phenomenon—as major as the Industrial Revolution.[1]

Due to economic necessity and to the Women's Movement with its emphasis on choice and self-fulfillment, women are returning to the work force in unprecedented numbers. The two-paycheck family has become a trend nationwide, and it is changing the family power structure and affecting lifestyles on a monumental scale. Its effects are reaching into all areas of life—including politics, leisure, finance, and the arts.

Alarmists are predicting disastrous results from this change away from traditional marriage patterns. They claim that men are losing jobs to women who shouldn't have them, that children are suffering from the lack of full-time mothers at home, and that damaged relationships are resulting in an increased divorce rate.

The evidence, however, is to the contrary. In fact, recent research indicates positive results from dual-career marriages. It seems that paid employment has very positive effects on both men and women, including building self-confidence and respect for one another. Apparently these traits are transferred from the workplace into our personal lives, and are significant in improving interpersonal relationships. In their recent book, *American Couples*, Philip Blumstein and Pepper W. Schwartz write:

> The demands of paid employment often push people to discover abilities they never knew they had. Once people develop self-confidence, they are not likely to want to give up such a new and rewarding sense of personal effectiveness when they come home from work.[2]

The first major research effort on the topic of dual-career marriages was undertaken by Catalyst, a non-profit organization that seeks to expand women's career options. In 1981, Catalyst released the report of their research—a two-pronged survey of 815 two-career couples and 374 major corporations. The survey results were direct and clear. Both husbands and wives indicated several advantages in combining career and family. Those which rated the highest included "more money," "autonomy for both," "growth," and "more security."[3]

Everything is not roses, however. Several disadvantages were reported in the Catalyst study. They included "not enough time together," "too much to do," "not enough leisure," and "too much pressure." When asked the question, "What would make the combination of career and marriage easier for you?" the respondents answered with a wide range of comments from "more time," and "more money," to "more household help," "childcare," and "better employment practices."[4]

Clearly, today's two-paycheck couple faces a whole new set of issues unknown to their parents or grandparents. For this new generation of dual-earner couples, there are no precedents, no guidelines to follow. This in itself, creates a difficult, but exciting challenge.

Salary and Power Equations

Although women are making great strides in the work force, their salaries still are not commensurate with those of their male counterparts. Recent statistics indicate that women are paid less than two-thirds as much as their male counterparts—about sixty-two cents for every dollar a man earns. For most couples this means an unequal distribution of wealth. Women may be putting the same amount of time and energy into their careers, but they are not bringing home the same incomes.

This situation leads to all kinds of power-related issues. If the man brings home a greater salary, should he be expected to share it completely with his wife? Should he be exempt from more of the household chores if he contributes a greater portion to the household expenses? What if he hires a cleaning person to do his half of the household chores and his partner can't afford to hire someone to do her half? If, in the same male-female relationship the situation is reversed and the wife's income is significantly greater, will both partners answer these questions the same way? If not, is something amiss?

Of course there are no clear-cut answers to these questions. What is absolutely essential, however, is that when negotiating these issues, both partners end up with a financial arrangement that is satisfactory. Furthermore, they both must feel free to open discussion and renegotiate any parts of the agreement at a future date.

The Time Crunch

Most dual-career couples indicate time as their single most pressing problem. There just are not enough hours in the day to devote to a career, relationship, children, and friends, to say nothing of exercise, hobbies, and chores. Often difficulties arise when partners are on different schedules or when one partner puts in longer hours than the other. Similarly, problems may arise when one person is out of town much more than the other.

How do successful couples handle the time crunch? Many have become experts in time-management techniques. They coordinate planning and keep up-to-date calendars. Along with scheduling time for meetings and social events, they also schedule time just to be together.

The following are time-management tips reported by couples who have been able to coordinate two careers successfully:

1. Make and use "to-do" lists for both work and home. Prioritize the lists and do the most important first. Whenever feasible, delegate the work.
2. Set aside blocks of time to accomplish important projects.
3. Use calendars diligently. Coordinate your calendar with your partner's. Use a joint calendar at home for scheduling social events, children's activities, and planned time together.
4. Plan time into your schedule for relaxation and for emergencies, perhaps an hour a day.
5. Purchase services that will save you time such as housecleaning, mowing, and yard work.
6. Cluster errands and run them on the way to or from work rather than making special trips. Use lunch hours to catch up on longer errands or shopping.

7. Sleep less. While this may not be a very appealing option, some couples report that by getting up an hour earlier each day they are able to get much more accomplished.
8. Watch TV less. It may be easier than giving up sleep!
9. Do two things at once: telephone and dishes, commute and dictate, television and letter-writing.
10. Develop routines that make your load lighter. Put in a load of wash every morning rather than letting it pile up for the weekend. Use a money machine on the way to work rather than waiting at the bank's drive-in branch after work.

Recognizing Flexibility and Rigidity in Scheduling

Recognizing the flexibility you have in your schedule may be the greatest key to controlling your time. While you may need to be at the office from nine to five on weekdays, you probably don't have to buy groceries on Saturday or do all the laundry on Sunday. Perhaps you can schedule an early morning breakfast meeting with your tennis-club committee and save your Thursday evening for playing bridge. Perhaps you can get your hair cut over a lunch break and save your after-work time for your child's soccer game.

If one partner has a more flexible schedule than the other, it will be easier to solve certain scheduling problems. This doesn't mean simply giving the person with the more flexible schedule the greater burden, but taking it into consideration when negotiating certain chores. For example, Bill and I finally resolved a longstanding conflict over grocery shopping in this manner: he buys all the perishable groceries and I buy all the non-perishable ones. Since my office is a fifty-minute drive from our house, I have never been able to pick up groceries on a lunch break. In the summer the ice cream would be completely melted by the time I got home; in the winter the lettuce and tomatoes would be frozen. With our new system I can buy groceries at noon on weekdays and avoid the weekend grocery-store crowds. Bill, who often works at our home, can more easily find the time to buy the perishable groceries and get them home before they thaw or spoil. So Bill and I have worked out a solution that makes use of his time flexibility without using him.

If there is a disparity in the flexibility of your schedules, or if there is a disparity in the number of hours which you put into your job per week, you may need to discuss this openly and resolve any conflict or resentment. The person with the lighter or more flexible workload may be willing to take on an extra portion of the chores, but it is important to make an up-front decision about this. Otherwise there can be resentment from both people.

If the person with the lighter load or more flexible schedule does agree to take on more, it should be negotiated in such a way that both people feel okay about the agreement. Also, any agreement should be open to renegotiation at any future point. I have found that in our relationship the pendulum has swung back and forth. I used to be home more than Bill, but currently I have a very long commute and an inflexible work schedule. Because of this, Bill gets stuck with certain responsibilities such as the rainy-day carpool for our first-grader and his neighborhood friends. Bill also stays home for repair and delivery people. I recognize and appreciate his efforts, and I attempt to compensate by doing telephone errands during work breaks at my office. I also do the lion's share of transporting our two youngest children to the babysitter's since I am going out anyway.

Buying Your Way Out—The Time/Money Trade-off

If you are in a two-paycheck marriage, you will soon begin to put a price tag on your time. Unless you enjoy it, it simply doesn't make sense to clip coupons and go to three or four grocery stores looking for bargains every week. Similarly, you may not want to refinish your grandma's rocker over the weekend. Or pick two bushels of peaches and can them for the winter.

At some point you may decide to buy canned peaches and hire someone to refinish the rocker. In making this decision you will want to consider if the activity itself is a source of satisfaction to you. If not, then can you afford to purchase the service? What are you willing to trade off to have the extra time or the extra money? As people move into higher income brackets, time is valued more and more. You may find yourself "buying" more time as the years pass.

But don't overlook the pleasures of some chores. Scott states, "I enjoy cooking sometimes and I enjoy vacuuming sometimes. These are mindless chores that give me a break during the week and sort of keep me in touch with my house and myself. Gardening is a specialized version of this. I might hire someone to mow the lawn, but I'd never hire anyone to weed the garden. It's low-level work but I like it. It's relaxing, connecting, and pleasurable."

There are many services and labor-saving devices on the market which can save incredible amounts of time if the chore is not particularly pleasant. You may not be able to afford them all, but even a few may help. My favorites include: cleaning person, microwave oven, telephone answering machine, lawn service, diaper service, and milk delivery. If I could afford it, I would have a live-in housekeeper—or a robot—who would take care of the laundry, grocery shopping, dry cleaning, all errands, babysitter scheduling, and most meals. I'd probably have the robot pack and unpack for vacations, also. I might even have it represent me at PTA meetings.

Childcare Issues

Lining up childcare can be one of the most frustrating parts of dual-career parenting. Unfortunately this country was unprepared for the large influx of women into the workplace in recent years. There are no standard procedures, policies or clearinghouses to provide assistance to parents needing childcare. The stories that couples relate often are appalling. Some of the difficulties, however, can be avoided if you and your partner go over your concerns and criteria for childcare and then conduct your search in an organized, systematic fashion.

First you will need to discuss what type of childcare best suits your needs. A babysitter coming into your home may seem to be the best situation. You avoid the inconvenience of transportation to a babysitter's house or daycare center at the beginning and end of each day. You also have someone in the house to do chores and get dinner started.

However, you will need to consider the cost and availability of such workers. Remember that anyone coming into your home to work full time can make more money doing just about anything else (and if so, why aren't they?). If you can find a good sitter to come to your house you're extremely fortunate, and you will be able to eliminate many of the nuisances that other couples face. But you do need to have backup arrangements in case the sitter calls in sick or has found another job.

The daycare home is a popular form of childcare, particularly for couples with infants or small children. Many couples feel that a family atmosphere is more appropriate than an institutional environment for very young children. Also, there are usually a few older children who can be playmates, not an oversupply as there might be at a daycare center, or a dearth as there might be at home.

Finding family daycare homes may be easy or difficult depending on your community. You may be able to obtain a listing of local family daycare homes from the Department of Social Services (or Office of Children's Services) usually administered by the county or state. Lamaze groups and other groups offering childbirth and parenting classes will frequently have phone numbers of offices in your area which provide listings of family daycare homes.

Often daycare homes are licensed. This means that they meet certain requirements for health and safety. You, however, will have to be the judge of the emotional, social, and educational aspects of the home. You will want to spend some time interviewing the caregivers in their own homes and observe their interactions with the children currently in their care. Be forewarned that there is a certain amount of subjectivity that will necessarily go into your choice. Your idea of a warm, loving atmosphere may be different from others', and it would be wise to look for an atmosphere which is consistent with that in your own home. Table 8.1 provides a checklist for interviewing babysitters and family daycare providers.

Table 8.1

**Checklist for Interviewing Babysitters
or Family Daycare Providers**

1. What is the person's general background? What kind of childcare experience has he or she had?
2. Are your workdays and hours in keeping with the sitter's?
3. What kind of structure will be provided for the children? Are certain times play time, meal time, nap time?
4. What are the sitter's views on discipline?
5. What are the sitter's opinions on children's eating habits? About toilet training? About naps? About television?
6. Does the sitter smoke? Drink?
7. What is the sitter's procedure for handling medical emergencies?
8. What areas of the house are play areas? What outdoor areas will be used for play? Are the play areas safe?
9. What are the sitter's fees? How are they to be paid?
10. How does the sitter interact with your child? Does s/he show an interest in your child? Does s/he talk to and hold your child during the interview? Does s/he show your child toys and talk about the other children? Does s/he seem genuinely interested in your child?
11. How does your child react to the sitter? Even non-verbal children will often give clues. Irritability or ill health such as stomach upsets may be a negative response.
12. What kinds of meals and snacks are typical?

Daycare centers are a third option for working parents. They range widely in philosophy, staff, and facilities. Many do not accept children until they are toilet-trained, although the number of centers accepting infants does seem to be growing. Usually you can find a comprehensive listing of daycare centers and nursery schools (many make a distinction between these labels) in the yellow pages under "Daycare Centers" and/or "Schools—preschools." Also you may want to check which centers provide day-long kindergarten, since many public school kindergartens are half-days, a problem for working parents. Table 8.2 provides a checklist of concerns when looking at preschools and daycare centers.

Many parents believe that once their children start school their daycare worries will end. Wrong. Daycare before and after school may be more difficult to find than full-time care. You do have some ready resources, however. Start first with the school to see if it provides before- and after-school programs; frequently larger schools will have such programs. Or there may be a before-school program, but no after-school program, or vice versa.

Table 8.2

Checklist for Comparing Nursery Schools and Daycare Centers

1. What are the center's goals? Is there an underlying philosophy or religious orientation?
2. How many staff members are there and how many children?
3. Are there structured programs for certain age groups? If so, what are they?
4. How is discipline handled?
5. Is there adequate space for many activities? Does there seem to be a variety of activities available?
6. What meals and snacks are provided? What would be a sample menu?
7. Are there outdoor activities planned? Is the outdoor play area safe and well-equipped?
8. Is the facility clean and safe?
9. How do the staff seem to be interacting with the children? With your child?
10. What are the hours and rates?
11. How much involvement do they expect from parents?
12. What is the policy about picking up a child late? Or when a child is sick?

If you are new to the neighborhood, your elementary school secretary may prove to be your best ally. He or she can let you know about official school programs and give you names of other two-paycheck parents who face similar scheduling problems. The secretary may also know of people in the neighborhood who can provide before- and after-school childcare. The current and past PTA presidents are other resources who usually know the neighborhood well and can provide information about childcare. Neighbors can help, too—along with the parents of your children's friends.

If you come to a dead end looking for traditional daycare in your neighborhood, try senior citizens, teenagers, or college students. Our first-grader goes to a sorority house around the corner from his school two mornings a week before school where a college student takes care of him. This arrangement works out well in that he is allowed to watch television until it is time for him to leave for school (a privilege he doesn't always have at home) and he gets lots of special attention from other sorority members too. If his sitter is sick or on vacation, one of her sorority sisters takes over.

Arranging Backups

You may be able to save both your job and your relationship by lining up backup childcare arrangements in advance of emergencies. It took Bill and me much too long to figure this out. After our first child was born I just assumed that if there were a problem with childcare one of us would stay home with the baby. Sounds simple, but of course, it isn't. Invariably the sitter will be sick on the days you both have impossible, demanding schedules that can't be altered. Also, it's unrealistic to assume that your sitter will only take vacations when you do. Sometimes you can coordinate this, but don't expect it to happen every year.

If you both are working in serious career-path positions, you *must* have backup childcare. I repeat, you *must* have backup childcare. Since you will be facing enough situations when your own children are sick, it's unwise to stay home when the sitter or her children are ill.

Of course, arranging substitute childcare is easier said than done. Many sitters simply don't want to be on call. Others, however, will be willing to take on last minute arrangements, if you meet with them and go over details in advance of any crisis.

You can find backup sitters in a number of ways. When you're interviewing for full-time sitters, your second and third choices might be possibilities. Your network of friends and associates is another resource. I found our first backup sitter by asking my hairdresser what sitter she used for her three daughters. Another of the backup sitters is the mother of a young man on my co-rec softball team. Another one came directly from the classifieds under "Childcare position wanted."

Emergencies at Home

Last minute emergencies tend to be the most difficult issues for dual-career couples to resolve, usually because immediate action is needed and there is so little time to work out the details. What do you do if ten minutes before you both are going to leave for work your daughter gets sick? Or the dog runs away? Or the kitchen faucet won't turn off? Or you discover the furnace isn't working? Chances are you hope that your partner's schedule will permit him or her to take care of it. But usually your partner is thinking the same thing, hoping you'll stay home and work things out.

There are no easy solutions in these situations, and many single people also have to deal with them. One first move is to assess the situation and determine your options. If your daughter is too sick for school, could she go to the babysitter's with her younger brother? Can you ask a neighbor to watch for Fido and take him in when he returns? Can you turn off the water supply to the house and deal with the faucet at the end of the day? Can you arrange for the furnace repair from your office and then take a late lunch or afternoon off to accommodate the repair person?

If there are no other alternatives than for one of you to stay home, then you need to do a quick review of your respective work schedules. Will one of you be putting your job in jeopardy by taking some personal time off? Does one of you have a more flexible schedule that particular day? Does one of you work considerably closer to home so that taking a half day off, or arriving late or leaving early is a possibility? Or can you split the responsibility with one of you taking off the morning, and the other the afternoon?

If no solutions emerge after considering these questions, then you can always consider who took care of the last crisis. Keep in mind, however, that this is a last-resort tactic. It simply makes sense to make your decision based on variables such as job flexibility rather than on a my turn/your turn basis. This may mean that you handle all the emergencies this year, but next year when you're in that new, high-pressured job, your partner will recognize the change and take care of the emergencies.

A Special Note on Sick Kids

A sick child is the one problem that dual-earner couples mention most. Somehow as forward-thinking individuals we are able to minimize the numbers of other emergencies by keeping our houses and cars in good repair. We also have backup systems for sick babysitters, transportation breakdowns, and school holidays. We keep in shape so that we ourselves don't get sick. But sick children are inevitable. And they always get sick on the worst possible day of the worst possible week of the worst possible month.

What can you do? Many times you have to bite the bullet and lose some time from work. However, it is possible to overreact. Here are some suggestions for dealing with sick kids.

1. Line up someone who knows your children well and is willing to care for them when they are slightly ill or recuperating. Make sure you pay this person appropriately. Sick kids are a big responsibility and require proper attention and lots of it. Make sure this person can reach you at all times, and that he or she has all the necessary medical information including doctors' numbers, preferred hospitals, medication, etc.
2. Don't immediately decide that the whole day is lost. Call in to work and report your situation and let them know you'll call back in an

hour. That way you can monitor your child and, if possible, go to work late or after lunch.

3. Work at home. If you are in a position to work on special projects, reports, or even routine activities, ask a co-worker to drop the material off at your house. While you still may have to report the day as "leave," you will stay abreast of your workload and not be swamped when you return.

4. Bring the child to work with you. Obviously you can do this only in a loosely structured work situation where you are in charge, and with a child who is only moderately sick. If you have any concerns that this would be poorly received by your co-workers or employees, stay home with the child.

The Six O'Clock Slump

Dinner time is the devil's time in most dual-earner households. Just when you come home exhausted and want nothing more than twenty minutes "downtime," you are faced with a similarly exhausted and irritable spouse, and perhaps one, two, or more whining, hungry children. Everyone has his or her own set of needs and no one pays particular attention to yours.

If you have no children, then you have more options to discuss with your partner. You may want a short nap. A workout at the club before dinner. Meditation in a cool, quiet basement. A late dinner out or a Chinese take-out rather than cooking.

If, however, you have children, it's a whole different ballgame. Then you'll have to compromise your needs for theirs. Depending on the ages of the children, you'll have various options. If the kids are very small you may need to fix an immediate dinner (immediate, not elaborate). Microwave ovens are marvelous for this. Otherwise you can give them a light snack such as carrot sticks or raisins to hold them over.

When both parents are working, evening meals cannot be formal or time-consuming. People don't need heavy meals at the end of the day anyway, so you will be contributing to your family's health if you have simple, light evening meals. The amount of energy you save from cooking and clean-up can go a long way toward other evening activities. If you reach the point of desperation, of course, you can call out to the various fast food places that deliver. You may discover that an Italian sub is a favorite meal, second only to pepperoni and mushroom pizza.

Some working couples have found routines that help with the six o'clock slump. Some put their kids in the bathtub as soon as they get home. It keeps the kids occupied for twenty to thirty minutes—just long enough to wind down from work. Others give the kids snacks and send them outside. Still others allow the television to be turned on—this even happens in households that limit TV viewing. "Whatever works, do it," seems to be the motto from the working couples I've interviewed. The six o'clock slump can be the most grueling time of the day and send an otherwise lovely evening tilting toward ruin. Do whatever it takes to beat the dinner hour madness and spare yourself, your spouse, your children (and maybe even the neighbors), a big headache.

Multiple Roles and Multiple Pleasures

Today much is being made of the new two-career couples and the stress involved in all the aspects of their lives—their jobs, their families, their friends, their individual interests. A plethora of books and articles is being published on the topic of juggling multiple roles, particularly for the working couple. Workshops abound on the topics of time- and stress-management, career- and self-development.

While the stress of managing multiple roles has received much attention, there is evidence that men and women alike respond positively to a multi-faceted lifestyle. Lois Verbrugge at the University of Michigan Institute for Social Research has conducted research which shows a positive association between multiple roles and good health. These roles include employment, marriage, and parenthood, with employment having the greatest impact.[5]

Verbrugge speculates that there may be a couple of reasons for this. Perhaps job and family ties offer much emotional support which enhances physical well-being. Or, perhaps healthier people simply choose to take on more roles. Whatever the reason, it is a positive finding for two-paycheck families.

Another factor not yet addressed in formal research is that multiple roles bring multiple satisfaction. Not only do you have a good job, but you have a fantastic spouse and children. All these are sources of pride and well-being.

Or, perhaps multiple roles offer a balance in our lives. If we fall short in one area, we can compensate in another. If the bookcase you're building for the den doesn't turn out as you'd planned, you can go to work and review your business successes. If your promotion at work doesn't come through, you can go home and watch your baby daughter take her first step. It may be that it is not only the successes in each of the roles that makes us happy and keeps us going, but also our ability to rationalize away the inevitable pain when we suffer losses in these roles.

While scheduling may seem endless and the pace may often seem too fast, two-paycheck couples do have the potential to achieve the best of all worlds. Perhaps multiple roles can mean multiple pleasures for both men and women.

Recommended Reading

Bird, Caroline. *The Two-Paycheck Marriage.* New York: Rawson Wade Publishers, 1979.

Hall, Francine E. and Douglas T. Hall. *The Two-Career Couple.* Reading, Mass.: Addison-Wesley Publishing Co., 1979.

Holmstrom, Lynda Lytle. *The Two-Career Family.* Cambridge, Mass.: Schenkman Publishing Co., 1973.

Ryglewicz, Hilary and Pat Koch Thaler. *Working Couples: How to Cope with Two Jobs and One Home.* New York: Simon and Schuster, 1980.

Shaevitz, Marjorie Hansen and Morton H. Shaevitz. *Making It Together as a Two-Career Couple.* Boston: Houghton Mifflin Co., 1980.

Footnotes

[1]Karen Barrett, "Two-Career Couples How They Do It," *MS,* Vol. XII, No. 12, June, 1984, p. 39.

[2]Philip Blumstein, Ph.D., and Pepper Schwartz, Ph.D. *American Couples.* (New York: William Morrow and Co., 1983), p. 141.

[3]"Corporations and Two-Career Families: Directions for the Future." (New York: Catalyst, 1981).

[4]Ibid.

[5]"Multiple Roles and Physical Health of Women and Men," *Journal of Health and Social Behavior,* Vol. 24, March, 1983, pp. 16–30.

9

Sex:
At His Fancy or Hers?

We talk about herpes at the dinner table. We view television advertisements for tampons and flavored douches without blinking. We nonchalantly pop the Pill. We've read all the sex manuals. We're so sophisticated, and yet we have so many sexual problems.

The media bombards us with the notion that sex is the culmination of the good life. If we wear the right jeans, drink the right Scotch, and drive the right car, the ultimate in sex is waiting—just around the corner.

We're also led to believe that every sexual encounter must end with the earth moving and bells ringing. We're out of luck if we don't know where to find the G-spot. If we don't have multiple simultaneous orgasms, something is amiss.

With these kinds of expectations it's no wonder that couples have problems. In our culture sex is promoted to the extreme. Sex is supposed to be wonderful, not only on warm, moonlit nights, but anytime without regard for the stress of the day—the hour-long traffic jam, the fight over the leftover pizza, or the baby crying in the next room. Sex, no matter what the circumstances, is supposed to be pure and utter bliss. Sex, in short, is overrated and overemphasized.

This is not to say that sex is unimportant; sex is an integral part of a good, primary relationship. Sex is playful, sex is joyous, sex is fun. It allows you to be intimate, trusting, and physically demonstrative. It's a wonderful way to enjoy a loving relationship.

Is Sex Really the Issue?

Frequently couples will come into a counseling session stating that they have a sexual problem. They may not have had sex in six months. Or the man is impotent. Or the woman is unsatisfied. Or any number of other concerns.

Sometimes these couples simply need to be taught how to communicate their sexual desires to one another. Or perhaps there is a medical problem that can be corrected. Or the couple may need to change their routine so that it is no longer an established pattern. However, for many of these couples, sex is only a surface issue. At the heart of the problem is a non-sexual matter—perhaps having to do with money, work, or children.

Sex problems are often linked with anger. One partner may be angry with the other and use sex as a means of hurting, distancing, or getting even with the other person. Ann and Marvin are an example. States Ann, "I used to get mad at Marvin for working such long hours—he spent very little time helping around the house or doing things with the kids. But instead of confronting him and telling him how mad I was, I just bit my lip. This affected our sexual relationship. I knew that it bothered his ego if he couldn't have an erection, so at some semi-conscious level, I would hold back or create a situation that was less than favorable for good sex. Part of me was pleased when he was impotent. I knew he was bothered by it, and I felt like I had gotten back at him."

Ann and Marvin's situation is not unusual. Couples frequently act out their anger and resentment in the bedroom. Fortunately, Ann and Marvin went into counseling and have resolved many of the overriding issues. Now they're both more straightforward about working out sexual and nonsexual problems. They're much more direct and honest with each other. If a problem arises, they're more inclined to deal with it at the time rather than letting it ride.

Similarly, Howard and Janine found their sex life foundering when Janine went back to work full time after being home with the children for seven years. Howard states, "When Janine decided to go back to work, I just assumed that she'd continue running the household. We didn't talk about it—her job offer came the first week she started looking—I didn't think either of us expected her to be working so soon. But once she started working she kept asking me to do things that I thought she should be doing, and the house was always a mess. She always claimed to be too tired from the new job to pick up the house and to have sex. We went for several months before we both decided our relationship was on the rocks if we didn't work something out."

Janine adds this to Howard's comments. "Running a household with two kids is a whole lot more work than doing it for two adults as I had done when we were first married and I was working full time. When I went back to work last March, I thought that Howard should split the chores—after all I was away at work as much as he was. The problem was that we never really discussed this with each other. We got angrier and angrier. Our sex life became non-existent. Finally when we did talk things out, we both saw how far apart our thinking was. I also think that it wasn't only the chores that affected our sex life. I simply was exhausted getting used to the new job. I started working at a bank and it was very stressful. One day on my first week someone withdrew $18,000 in cash—I had to go into a little room and count it all out and hope that I was accurate so that the accounts balanced at the end of the day. Now that I'm used to the job, I don't come home frazzled like I did those first few weeks. We've worked out a plan for splitting up the chores, and sex is even better than it used to be. I think the self-confidence I've gained from going back to work has helped a lot."

A younger couple, Deborah and Aaron had a problem with finances that found its way into the bedroom. Deborah explains, "After we got married we had quite a bit of wedding money. Aaron and I talked about getting another car—he wanted a jazzy sports car. I was interested in saving it for a down payment on a house when we finished school, and we talked about that, too. One day after we had talked about the car again, Aaron came home and said he had gone ahead and ordered one—it had fewer frills than what he wanted but that left a little money to save for the house. I was furious, but I was afraid to make an issue of it so I said okay. But let me tell you there was no way I was going to make love with him after that. It took a few weeks without sex and a few more of counseling before we got back on track again."

The experiences of these couples serve to illustrate that if left unresolved, non-sexual issues can turn into sexual ones. When non-sexual issues are at the root of a relationship problem, it is imperative that they be recognized and worked out. If the real issues are money, work, household chores, children, or in-laws, they should be negotiated with the goal of establishing win-win outcomes. Without such a process, sex is only a surface issue, and there's little hope for its improvement.

If you're fighting or feeling angry with one another, for whatever reason, it can sour your sexual relationship. If you sense that the real underlying issues are not sexual ones, start negotiating the non-sexual areas first. Once you resolve those problems, you'll be in a much more positive frame of mind to negotiate and improve your sexual relationship.

Learning to Talk Openly About Sexual Issues

Sex is such a loaded topic that it is understandably difficult for many couples to broach in open, honest conversation. However, this is a necessary first step in improving a sexual relationship. Inhibitions can be overcome. You need to put forth some effort to express yourselves clearly and be sensitive to each other's discomfort.

Reading some books on the topic of sexuality may be useful in providing information about what is within the range of normal sexual behavior. Books like *The Joy of Sex* and *More Joy of Sex* can provide you with the necessary vocabulary to discuss your particular needs and interests. In fact, these two books have a dictionary format which defines terms with clear, thorough descriptions. Consult the Recommended Reading section for other resources.

Table 9.1, Communicating Your Sexual Concerns with Your Partner, also may aid you in breaking down the barriers to communication on this important topic. As you go through this exercise, be sure to let your partner know what is difficult for you to discuss. That way he or she can be sensitive to your concerns and make it easier.

Table 9.1

**Communicating Your Sexual Concerns
with Your Partner**

List the areas in which you feel positive about your sexual relationship.

List the areas in which you would like to make changes.

List specific things you would like your partner to do (or not do) when you are having sex.

List any other areas of concern regarding your sexual relationship.

Marriage counselors and sex therapists also can aid couples in communicating their sexual needs and desires to each other. Once you feel free to talk, you can indicate to your partner what times and places you find most stimulating, and what items are "turn-ons" and "turn-offs."

Sex as a Substitute for Intimacy

People need warm, intimate, close physical contact with other people. Research with infants indicates that those who establish close bonds with their parents at birth and continue to have much cuddling, holding, and attention, have a higher survival rate than those who don't. From birth until death we have a basic need to be physically close to other people.

Unfortunately there are cultural taboos against physical contact. Except for babies and small children, it is not socially acceptable to touch, hug, or cuddle each other in public or in private. The one major exception, of course, is sex. With sex it's okay to touch, fondle, and caress each other.

Sex, in our society, has become just about the only avenue to enjoy physical closeness. Our culture allows women, to some degree, to be close to other women. But even that allows only for an occasional embrace or quick kiss on the cheek. Our culture permits men even less physical contact—shaking hands, or an occasional touch in a sports activity, but certainly no warm, open, totally physical, non-sexual encounters. It's not surprising, then, that sex has taken on such enormous dimensions. Because people crave physical closeness and touching, sex gains a prominence that it would not have in an environment open to touching and physical contact.

Many clients indicate to Bill and me that what they most enjoy about sex is the touching and cuddling. Sex in itself is not so important as the physical intimacy, being close to each other. What this means, of course, is that they are using sex as a means of achieving this universal human need for physical closeness. There is nothing inherently wrong in that. But it does illustrate how much we are limiting ourselves if we choose only sex to achieve this type of intimacy.

In the book *Touching*, Ashley Montagu cites several cases in which individuals report using sex as a means of being held and cuddled. He states:

> . . .in the Western world it is highly probable that sexual activity, indeed the frenetic preoccupation with sex that characterizes Western culture, is in many cases not the expression of sexual interest at all, but rather a search for the satisfaction of the need for contact.[1]

Montagu points out that many people who have inadequate stroking, caressing, and cuddling during infancy and childhood may as adults have difficulty with tactile awareness and sexual issues.

Recognizing this basic human need for physical intimacy, it is important to allow yourself and your partner to be close and touch each other without sex. You may want to cuddle or lie together while relaxing at home watching television or listening to music. You may want to cuddle together every evening before you go to sleep or every morning when you awaken. Once you take care of your need for physical contact, sex will have both a lesser and greater significance. Lesser in that it will not be as pressing a need, and greater in that the desire for sex will be just that. Sex will likely be improved—more fervent and impassioned—once you've already achieved your daily quotient of T.L.C.

Ground Rules

A first step in establishing a good sexual relationship is negotiating the ground rules. These include questions such as who can initiate sex, when, where, and with what kind of frequency. While these questions cannot be answered with total precision, it's a good idea to discuss your general expectations and anything you or your partner might consider outside the norm.

The biggest question you face, however, is that of fidelity. Do you want to have sex outside your primary relationship? If so, what are the parameters? How will you know if it's not working? What kind of constraints do you want to add?

The Question of Fidelity

In an age when sexual fidelity may seem old-fashioned, I think it is requisite for couples who want to build a solid, lasting relationship. In the long run the benefits far outweigh any pleasure gained through an outside affair. It is not in any right-wrong moralistic sense that I advocate not having outside sex, it is from a purely pragmatic point of view. Couples don't break up as a result of fidelity. Infidelity, however, frequently causes break-ups and almost always much guilt and pain.

Consider the following reasons for making a firm and overt "No Outside Sex" agreement with your partner.

1. *There's more freedom to be close to others.* If you're clearly committed to a sexual relationship only with your partner, you can pursue close friendships (of either sex) without concern that you'll get involved or that your partner will be jealous. In a real sense this means that you can develop close friendships without fear of sexual overtones. It also means unlimited possibilities for cultivating other friendships. You can enjoy a friend of the opposite sex as a jogging partner, lunch or dinner date, concert companion, or bridge partner

without a moment's hesitation. You can go swimming together, go to a movie, ride horses, or take a walk through the zoo—all at no risk to your primary relationship.

2. *If you have a firm commitment to your partner, it's easier to say no to others.* Assuming you're reasonably friendly and attractive, someone is bound to make an advance at some time. It may be someone you like a lot and in other circumstances you might accept the advance. If you have an agreement not to have outside sex, you need not expend any energy on an agonizing decision. Your refusal is much easier. You have made a firm, up-front agreement with your partner and it is important not to break it. You also can take comfort in the knowledge that your partner, when faced with a similar situation, will also refuse.

3. *Jealousy is a dead issue.* If you have an agreement of fidelity, then you needn't be suspicious or jealous, knowing that your partner is solidly committed to you. You are number one in your partner's life.

4. *You spare your partner and yourself the immense pain which so frequently accompanies infidelity.* It is easy to talk about the monotony of monogamy and contrast it with the excitement of a sexually open relationship. But the reality may be very different from the fantasy. Too often people discover too late that they are not the free flowing, sexually liberated individuals they once thought they were. After acknowledging the partner's infidelity they find themselves subject to overwhelming jealousy, anger, and outrage.

5. *You don't risk the trust and commitment you have given to each other.* Since trust and commitment are at the heart of any enduring relationship, you don't threaten these important values. While it is possible to rebuild that lost trust and commitment, it is usually a painstakingly slow process which may take several years.

This is not to say that enjoying different sexual partners is wrong. Sexual experimentation with various partners may make sense for many people—particularly young people who are still dealing with questions of self-identity and who are not ready to begin a primary relationship. In these situations enjoying a wide variety of partners and experiences may aid in self-discovery. It also has a secondary benefit in that later on, once established in a primary relationship, an individual may not have regrets about being faithful to one partner. If you've already tasted the grass on the other side of the fence, it may not seem one bit greener.

The Details

Other details you may need to work out include the frequency and length of sexual activity you both prefer. You may also want to consider time and places—particularly if you and your partner seem to have different sexual "clocks." You may need to work out compromises, one time satisfying your partner's desires, another time satisfying your own, or compromising both of your preferences in one session.

Telling Your Partner What You Want

The single most important key to a good sexual relationship is the ability to communicate with your partner—both verbally and nonverbally. While this may sound simple, for many people it's not. You must be able to tell your partner what pleases you, and your partner must be able to do the same.

Sometimes making a list is useful. Table 9.2 illustrates Charlie and Julia's individual "I Want" lists. They both wrote down a list of what they wanted in order to enjoy sex more. Then they went over the lists together.

Table 9.2
Charlie and Julia's "I Want" Lists

Charlie	Julia
I want hot passionate sex, with Julia losing all reserve.	I want to be told I'm beautiful.
I want Julia to initiate oral sex with me.	I want to be kissed all over from head to toe.
I want to try new positions and new gimmicks.	I want sex to last longer than ten minutes—I'm tired of "quickies."

In discussing their desires, Charlie and Julia soon discovered that they each wanted the other to take the more active role, Julia wanting to be kissed by Charlie, and Charlie wanting Julia to initiate lovemaking with fellatio. They also discovered that Julia was interested in foreplay—especially caressing—and wanted that extended longer. Charlie was more eager to move into impassioned intercourse. After a lengthy discussion they decided they could meet each other's needs. They would alternate being the initiator and both would consider each other's desires.

Once they saw each other as making an effort to meet the other's needs, Julia and Charlie found that their sexual relationship improved. Both began to enjoy other styles of lovemaking. They both became more assertive about initiating sex. They still had an occasional "quickie" but more often than not their lovemaking has been longer and colored with more variety.

Initiating Sex

Research indicates that couples who can initiate and refuse sex on an equal basis are more satisfied with their sex lives.[2] If you don't feel free to initiate sex with your partner, you need to discuss this subject with him or her. What are the reasons? Does your partner encourage or discourage you from initiating sex? How can you get over your inhibitions? What can your partner do to help?

This discussion should help you become more sexually assertive. You may find, however, that your partner will need to support you in overcoming some inhibitions. Because you both have so much to gain, it makes sense to look at this as a mutual concern. Perhaps changing your usual time and place for lovemaking would help you to break away from old, established patterns. Frequently, a weekend away or a full-blown second honeymoon will provide a setting conducive to changing roles.

Saying No

A critical factor in improving your sex life is giving each other permission to say no. This means not only saying the word to each other, but really meaning it and abiding by it. It also means accepting the no without feeling hurt or rejected.

A carryover from another age that many of us still live with, is the expectation that a woman must always be ready at her partner's beck and call. This kind of situation obviously is a set-up for passive and uninteresting, hurried sex. For many women, not being able to say no has meant enduring sex and getting it over with as soon as possible.

Men also have suffered the consequences of Victorian standards. Maintaining a "macho" stereotype, men are always supposed to be powerful and sexually aggressive. However, today, when women take over some initiating, men frequently feel that they can't say no, believing that it is part of their masculine image to be sexually hungry at all times. This can result, for example, in headaches, depression, or impotence.

Permission to say no has a liberating effect. If both partners truly feel comfortable saying no, then their odds for truly satisfying sexual experiences are greatly increased. If you can say no, then you don't have to fake enjoyment. If you can say no, they you don't have to do it half-heartedly. If you can say no, then you can be sure that your partner is doing it because he or she truly wants to share the experience with you.

Simply giving each other permission to refuse, however, isn't enough. It means carrying out the agreement without guilt, shame, hostility, or rejection. It means understanding that if your partner refuses your advances, the decision comes from within him or her, not from you. Frequently both men and women have a lot of trouble coping if their sexual advances are turned down. They interpret it as a rejection of themselves, and hang on to hurt and angry feelings. *It is absolutely imperative that you not let this happen.*

If you feel rejection after your partner has turned down your suggestion, be realistic. Sometimes you're not always in the mood either. Perhaps your partner's job or other responsibilities have drained him or her of emotion and energy. Perhaps your partner wants the time to do something else. There are any number of valid reasons why your partner would say no. If in doubt, check it out. Chances are he or she isn't in the mood. Sometimes you won't be in the mood either, and you will be appreciative that no is okay.

Sexual Negotiations

While negotiating sex may sound laughable, in fact, it's not. Often sexual issues are best communicated and resolved in a logical, straightforward method. Working from the assumption that both you and your partner have basic needs, it is important to communicate them to each other and work out mutually agreeable compromises. If she wants wine and candlelight and he wants X-rated movies, there can be room for both.

The bedroom, however, may not be the best place for this discussion. A more neutral area is much better. That way you don't have any "performance" pressures. Writing about this issue, Alexandra Penney, author of *How to Make Love to Each Other* states, "Bed is usually *not* a good place to discuss problems as it seems to put many people on the defensive. Some couples I talked with find that sitting around the kitchen table with a cup of coffee or tea is 'neutral' yet intimate and comfortable territory."[3] For the best results, choose a place outside the bedroom that is neutral, quiet, and private.

Not only where you choose to negotiate sexual issues, but *how* is of extreme importance. Because this is such a sensitive topic with much ego involvement, it must be approached carefully. The emphasis necessarily should be win-win. If you approach your partner in a positive, loving manner with concerns about him or her, the result is much more likely to be positive than if you focus only on your own needs. With sex, all solutions must be win-win; there's no win-lose. If one of you loses in a sexual relationship, you both lose. Loving, joyous sex requires a positive attitude from both partners and both gain in the love and joy which results.

Recommended Reading

Braun, Saul, editor. *Catalog of Sexual Consciousness*. New York: Grove Press, Inc., 1975.

Castleman, Michael. *Sexual Solutions*. New York: Simon and Schuster, 1980.

Comfort, Alex, M.B., Ph.D. *The Joy of Sex*. New York: Simon and Schuster, 1973.

——— *More Joy of Sex*. New York: Simon and Schuster, 1973.

Penney, Alexandra. *How to Make Love to Each Other*. New York: Berkley Books, 1982.

Sarrel, Lorna J., M.S.W., and Philip M. Sarrel, M.D. *Sexual Turning Points*. New York: Macmillan Publishing Company, 1984.

Westheimer, Ruth. *Dr. Ruth's Guide to Good Sex*. New York: Warner Books, 1983.

Footnotes

[1]Ashley Montagu, *Touching* (New York: Harper & Row, 1971), p. 192.

[2]Philip Blumstein, Ph.D., and Pepper Schwartz, Ph.D. *American Couples* (New York: William Morrow, 1983), p. 222.

[3]Alexandra Penney, *How to Make Love to Each Other* (New York: Berkley Books, 1982), p. 132.

10

Vacations: Where Do We Go from Here?

Just about everyone has fantasized the perfect vacation. Usually it is in an idyllic setting—sailing to an exotic Greek island, sipping wine at a Parisian cafe, or taking a safari through the wilds of Kenya. Never, however, does the fantasy include children screaming in the back seat of the car during the first hour of your 2,000-mile trip from Minneapolis to San Francisco. Fantasy vacations do not include two-hour lines at amusement parks, "no vacancy" signs at motels and camp sites, or the need for Pepto-Bismol. While most of us have experienced these troubles while traveling, many of us may still be waiting to fulfill our dream vacations.

John, currently divorced, tells a story of his early married days when his wife planned a family vacation. Living on a shoestring with two young children, their only financial option was a camping trip. Neither of them had had any experience camping. What she wanted was a romantic evening under the stars while the children slept peacefully in the tent. The first evening out they gave up on the half-burnt steaks, and settled into a leaky tent with crying children and huge mosquitoes. The vacation ended the next day with many bitter feelings.

While John's vacation tale is pitiful, he now views it with humor and is able to realize that the problem was not so much the experience itself, but the couple's lack of realistic planning. Not being familiar with the routines of camping, they had not planned for the contingencies of rain, faulty equipment, or mosquitoes. Also, they were not able to laugh off the event and try again at a different time and place.

Despite the problems endemic to vacations, plenty of couples do enjoy fantasy vacations. They come home with stories of the marvelous beauty of the Canadian Rockies, delectable meals in New Orleans, and double rainbows in Hawaii. What makes their experiences different? If, in fact, they are not covering up for a miserable week suffering from altitude sickness in Banff, getting mugged during the Mardi Gras, or fighting the crowds at Waikiki, they may have come to some common agreements regarding when, where, and especially *how* to spend their vacations.

Psychological Vacation Needs

The greatest contributor to ruined vacations is not bad weather, but differing expectations. If one partner wants a quiet, relaxing getaway, while the other wants to pack as much excitement as possible into an eighteen-hour day, then obviously there will be a conflict.

Usually the differences are not so extreme. One husband may be viewing a weekend in New York as an opportunity to shop for cameras and electronic equipment. His wife, however, may have in mind museums, plays, and fancy restaurants. In this situation plenty of compromises are available. There will be a problem, however, if the couple fails to communicate their desires and does not work out a mutual plan prior to the trip.

The popular magazine, *Psychology Today*, surveyed its readers a few years ago on the topic of how Americans view vacations. They had more than 10,000 responses and summarized the findings in the May 1980 issue. Six vacation needs emerged from that survey: relieving tension, intellectual enrichment, family togetherness, exotic adventure, self-discovery, and escape. The majority of the respondents reported their reasons for taking vacations included the need for rest and relaxation, and a means of escaping their regular routines. Others indicated using vacations as opportunities to visit friends and relatives, to recharge and be renewed, and to explore new places.[1]

These various vacation needs are listed in Table 10.1. Before planning a vacation together as a couple, I suggest that both partners rank their own individual vacation needs using the table. After both have completed the exercise, discuss the differences.

A word of caution here! You could be defining the terms differently. Be sure to discuss what "escape" or "self-discovery" means to each of you. For example, escape could be escape from your work, your children, your creditors, or even your partner. Similarly, self-discovery could mean time alone to contemplate one's past and future, or a trip back to the land of one's origin, or a weekend workshop with a noted psychologist.

Table 10.1

Your Vacation Needs

Relieve Tension

Intellectual Enrichment

Family Togetherness

Exotic Adventure

Self-Discovery

Escape

Each partner should separately rank his or her psychological priorities for vacations. Then compare rankings and discuss how these needs can be met with different kinds of vacations.

The psychological needs are taken from a *Psychology Today* survey summarizing the responses of 10,000 Americans. The six listed above emerged as the top vacation needs. *Psychology Today*, May, 1980, pp. 62–66.

Likewise, if your partner and you find that you have different psychological needs at the top of your respective lists, it does not necessarily mean that both of your needs cannot be met in the same vacation. For example, if intellectual enrichment is your top priority, and family togetherness is your partner's top priority, there may be many ways to combine the two.

Bill and I were able to work out this kind of vacation a couple of years ago. I was very involved in gathering information about one of my ancestors who was a Union soldier in the Civil War. From a collection of family letters and some regimental histories, I was able to determine the battles in which he had fought and where his company had camped. I then became excited about retracing his footsteps in some campaigns in northern Virginia.

Bill humored me about my excitement, but agreed on the trip to Virginia because we would also be visiting some special friends in the area. We had a good visit with our friends, and Bill especially enjoyed that part of the vacation. When we got to the battlefields, to my surprise, Bill also found himself getting interested in the Civil War. Our children were pre-schoolers and too young to appreciate the historical perspective of the vacation, but they liked being outdoors in the country, and having the freedom to run around at will. They also seemed to enjoy the exhibits at the war museums. We had a lot of fun together as a family, and the trip satisfied my curiosity about my relative's role in the Civil War.

Another useful tool in sorting out more specific priorities is Table 10.2, the Vacation Styles chart. You may find that you have differences in your expectations regarding the pace of the trip, the amount of time you spend together or alone, the amount of structure built into the day, and other items such as luxury vs. budget accommodations. Again, you may choose to negotiate the differences and end up with a compromise that you can both enjoy. Or you may choose to separate yourselves more than usual once you reach your destination.

Table 10.2

Vacation Styles

Your vacation priorities will change depending on your lifestyle, work environment, and prior vacations. Label your priorities:

A = Very Important   B = Somewhat Important   C = Not Important

Fast-paced
Relaxed
Time together
Time alone
Unscheduled time
Scheduled activities
Scenic beauty
Metropolitan environment
Outdoor activities
Luxury accommodations
Sightseeing
Special interests (e.g., jazz festival, ethnic fair)
Self-improvement (e.g., weight-loss resort)
Sports or Fitness (e.g., golf, jogging, tennis)
Other

After prioritizing, compare with your partner. Discuss both similar and dissimilar priorities.

Carol and Sheldon had to work out a compromise when they discovered they had different priorities for their summer vacation. Sheldon said that he wanted to go to the Rocky Mountains spending time hiking and enjoying the scenery. He also said that he didn't like stuffy resorts where you have to dress for dinner; he wanted the flexibility to be able to move on at a moment's notice. Carol, on the other hand, had different concerns. She said that where they went was not so important as the opportunity to be away from the children for parts of the day. She said a resort or hotel with childcare arrangements would be her top choice. She said she wanted both time to share activities with the family and time to be alone.

When they started their negotiation session, Carol and Sheldon made a list of areas that were not in conflict. They included (a) taking the children, (b) going to the Rocky Mountains, and (c) hiking. The areas of conflict included (a) resort vs. stop-and-go traveling, and (b) finding childcare (which was not compatible with stop-and-go traveling).

Their compromise was one week of stop-and-go traveling in Colorado, and one week at a casual dude ranch in the Rocky Mountains. Childcare was available at the ranch, as were a variety of activities including hiking. Because the dude ranch was so casual and offered a number of trails to explore, Sheldon did not object as he might have to a more formal East Coast resort. Because childcare was available at the ranch, Carol was willing to do without it during the other week on the road.

When discussing your psychological vacation needs with your partner, you may find that you actually are at loggerheads with no compromise in view. If you want a quiet, relaxing vacation to relieve you from the tension of work and family life, and your partner wants the adventure of sky-diving into the Grand Canyon, there may be no middle ground. Perhaps you could go along with your partner and not participate in the sky-diving yourself, but if you do that and find yourself worrying about your partner's safety, you've defeated your purpose. In that case you need to (a) negotiate with your partner for a different vacation altogether, or (b) schedule separate vacations.

Timing

If your vacation time is limited to two or three weeks a year, I would strongly recommend outlining tentative plans at the beginning of the year. Many working couples need to do this out of necessity, in order to schedule vacation time at work. If you have children, you will probably want to consider school holidays and summer vacations as well.

Table 10.3, the Yearly Vacation Planner, may aid you in determining the number of vacations and long weekends you take, along with which other people (if any) you will include. Also, if you have limited vacation time, it will enable you to see how many short vacations or long weekends you can fit in, in addition to a long vacation. Filling out the Yearly Vacation Planner may also help you to spend your time doing what you want to do, where you want to do it, and with whom, rather than simply waiting until you get an invitation for a weekend away.

Table 10.3

Yearly Vacation Planner

Total Vacation Time: __15__ Weekdays + __8__ Holidays Weekdays = __23__ Total

	LONG VACATION	SHORT VACATION	LONG WEEKEND	TIME OFF AT HOME
ALONE			Visit Deb in New York in October	2 or 3 days in Spring for odd jobs.
WITH PARTNER			Mackinac Island in August Washington D.C. in May	
WITH CHILDREN	Ten days Camping trip in Smokey Mtns. (over 4th of July)	Visit Chicago relatives between Christmas + New Year's		Home on New Year's, Memorial Day Labor Day Thanksgiving + Christmas
WITH FRIENDS			Cross-country ski in January Toronto in March	

To use the Yearly Vacation Planner, start out by adding up the number of weekdays you will receive in vacation time; add in any weekday holidays you would like to use for vacation (e.g., Memorial Day, Fourth of July, Labor Day). With that total you have a working number to sketch out your vacation plans for the year. It is a good idea to build in some slack for unexpected opportunities.

While filling in the Vacation Planner, it makes sense to take into consideration time that you or your partner will be out of town as part of your work, attending conferences, conventions, etc. While this may not count as vacation time, time away from home definitely affects your desire to travel on your own time. You simply may not want to take a vacation a week after you return from a conference in Miami in January; you may, however, desperately need a warm Florida vacation by the middle of March.

The Right People

Another consideration when filling out your Yearly Vacation Planner is whether to go alone, with your partner, with your children, or with friends. These decisions undoubtedly will change as your life situation changes. Because our children are young, ages six, three, and one, Bill and I prefer to take weekends off by ourselves, rather than spend extended periods away from the children. However, our friends with teenagers and grown children find it much easier to be away from their children for a couple of weeks at a time.

With Children

Vacationing with small children may be an endurance test. While ten- and twelve-year-olds may make ideal traveling companions, the baby to five-year-old set can be very trying. Go well-prepared with snacks, toys, and surprise diversions. Plan plenty of playtime and breaks, and utilize public parks and playgrounds. Always plan about twice as much time as you think you'll need for feedings, diaper changes, play periods, and scoldings. If you are going by car, take a cassette tape player with plenty of cassette stories and songs (usually available at a public library in the children's section). Small children will sit still and listen to these songs and stories when nothing else will work to keep them quiet. Also consider picnics and fast food restaurants as alternatives to fancier restaurants where children are expected to be quiet and sit still.

Older children can be delightful travelers, particularly if they are involved in the planning process. Some children take pleasure in leading the family on tours of certain historic sites that they have studied in school. They also enjoy map-reading, planning side trips, and seeking out motels and restaurants. Older children, however, also get tired and bored, grouchy, and absolutely unreasonable when traveling.

The best advice I can give for traveling with children is to be flexible and not expect perfection. If you have to find a restroom ten minutes after you've left the restaurant, accept it with a sense of humor and insist that everyone use the restroom at the next stop. You can also expect several knock-down drag-out fights, and at least one child throwing up along the way. If that doesn't happen, you're beating the odds.

With Friends

Vacationing with friends also has potential for extreme success or disaster. Before embarking on a trip with friends, it is important to get a clear idea of their priorities and expectations. Setting a specific itinerary and setting aside time to pursue separate interests will probably add to the success of the trip. If you are having any hesitation about vacationing with a particular couple or individual, my general rule of thumb is *don't.* Personality characteristics which may be slightly irritating in a regular relationship are likely to be magnified on a vacation. Certainly never commit to a long trip with friends before testing out a weekend or short trip together.

Alone

Contrary to popular belief, separate vacations can be an indication of a healthy relationship. Fortunately, in the past few years they have become socially acceptable. Taking a vacation alone can give you a chance to break away from your usual routine, catch your breath, and reflect on issues which are important to you alone. In this situation you can do exactly what you want on your own schedule without meeting anyone else's demands. You may find that you are lonely. However, you may find that a vacation by yourself is a refreshing interlude.

Every year I take a long weekend and visit my friend Deb in New York. It is a time to renew our friendship, catch up on the year's activities, and share intimacies. We take long walks, go to plays, and eat at wonderful New York restaurants. If Bill were to come along, I am sure that he would be bored and feel left out. It works much better for him to stay home and take his separate trip to see the Chicago Cubs play at his favorite ballpark, Wrigley Field. For Bill and me, it's a win-win arrangement that satisfies both of us.

Vacation Budgeting

It's critical that both partners have an understanding of their vacation budget before embarking on a trip. Use the household budget form in chapter 3 to aid you in getting started. Then allocate the total among the various trips and weekends you are planning for the year. You may then choose to use Table 10.4, the Daily Vacation Budget Planner, in estimating your daily expenditures for food, lodging, transportation, sightseeing, souvenirs, etc. This process may guide you in the amount you have to spend for accommodations, meals, and added extras.

Table 10.4

Daily Vacation Budget Planner

Total Allocated for Entire Trip	$ _____
Deduct Transportation Expenses	_____
Balance	$ _____

Divide Balance by Number of Days = Total Daily Budget

$$\$ \underset{\text{Balance}}{\underline{\hspace{2cm}}} \div \underset{\text{Days}}{\underline{\hspace{2cm}}} = \$ \underset{\text{Daily Budget}}{\underline{\hspace{2cm}}}$$

Or Allocate:

Lodging	$ _____
Food	_____
Sightseeing	_____
Entertainment	_____
Local Transportation	_____
Souvenirs/Shopping	_____
Emergency Reserve	_____
Other	_____
Total Daily Budget	$ _____

Budget vs. Luxury

The issue of budget vs. luxury is a personal one. Some couples would forgo a three-week budget trip for a one-week luxury one. Other couples would always opt for the longer, cheaper version.

Camping, of course, is the usual budget vacation. To be a camper, however, takes a particular sort of individual who can tolerate dirt, cramped quarters, cold, and rain, in exchange for the obvious benefits of savings, flexibility in traveling, and closeness to nature. However, there are many levels within camping. A spotless, well-furnished motor home in Pompano Beach is obviously in a different league from back-packing at Third Recess Lake, a three-day, uphill climb in the Sierras.

Most campers test out the experience by renting or borrowing equipment before purchasing their own. That's an excellent idea, and one that Bill and I *did not* utilize a few years ago. We now have snow-camping equipment, used only once on an excruciatingly cold, twenty-below-zero Michigan night. See Table 10.5.

Table 10.5

Tips from Seasoned Travelers

1. Don't forget to pack medication, including birth control.
2. Try out all new equipment before leaving.
3. Take extra money for emergencies.
4. Take reading materials, games, and cards for long waits.
5. Be aware of local holidays and bank closings.
6. Take only carry-on luggage (on flights).
7. Expect rain.

Luxury vacationing is another story. This is when you expect to be treated like a king and queen and pay for it. Luxury vacations can be a wonderful reward to yourself for a special accomplishment, or for no other reason than simply being a special person.

Beware, however, of feeling guilty or too stressed to enjoy the luxury. Not everything will go perfectly, so expect 90 percent and feel okay about the 10 percent which goes awry. If you're on a cruise, give yourself permission to pass up prepaid meals if your stomach is upset. Or if you're at a tennis camp, let yourself skip the pre-breakfast lesson if you want to sleep in.

Enjoy being pampered. You may even want to give yourself a little extra such as a massage from the hotel masseuse, breakfast from room service, or a corsage for the concert. These extra touches often become the special memories of the trip.

Visiting Relatives

Pat and Bob take their two children and visit her parents in Charleston every year. In the early years they drove the family car; in recent years they have flown. Pat's parents are pleasant people, and Charleston is a lovely city with a variety of attractions. Every year both Pat and Bob expect the vacation to be a pleasure, and it is.

Pat and Bob's situation, unfortunately, is not the norm. According to dozens of couples I interviewed collecting data for this book, a common bone of contention is that of obligatory trips to visit relatives. Many spouses are irritated at being forced to use precious vacation time on stressful, unpleasant visits to the in-laws.

Interestingly, in many situations, it is not the spouse but the adult child who reacts negatively to these obligatory visits. "Even though I'm thirty years old my parents still treat me like a kid," is a comment frequently heard from such disgruntled children. Somehow people often can cope with their in-laws much better than with their own parents.

Many of the couples I interviewed had worked out compromises or creative solutions to the obligatory visits to relatives. For example:

1. *Combine the visit with another trip* so that you spend a few days at the beginning or end of the trip with the relatives—not the entire vacation.

2. *Go separately on occasion,* particularly if you don't need your spouse for emotional support in dealing with your relatives.

3. *Go less frequently.* This suggestion was made most often by grown children whose parents expected them to visit on all the traditional holidays as well as in the summer. That kind of frequency may not be necessary or reasonable.

4. *Spend fewer days when you do visit.* Terry, a therapist, relates a problem of one of his clients. The client would visit his out-of-state parents faithfully for two weeks every year. Each year he was miserable for the entire two weeks. When Terry suggested he cut the visit down to three or four days, the client protested that the flight was so expensive that he could only justify the cost for a two-week visit. At that, Terry retorted, "So, it's better to pay that much money for fourteen days of misery than for three or four." The client had not thought about it in those terms and decided to try a shorter stay.

5. *Pay their expenses to come to you.* This is a particularly good option for retired parents who have more free time. Also the rail and bus systems often offer senior citizen rates which may be much less costly than if you were to travel yourself. With this option you also save on travel time. In addition, you may be able to work during part of their visit, on days they would like some quiet time at home, or on days they would prefer to go off sightseeing or shopping. This way you can use fewer vacation days and still have the enjoyment of their company. This kind of visit may prove to be more enjoyable for parents, too, in that it is likely to be slower paced with more frequent quiet periods, and less round-the-clock interaction with one another.

Special Interests/Special Needs

It's likely that as a couple you will develop your own individual style of vacationing. You may find yourselves returning to a favorite resort year after year; or conversely, you will set out every year to explore unknown territory.

You may choose to share every minute together, or you may choose to go your own way the moment you reach your destination.

Fran and Larry have worked out some excellent compromises in their mode of vacationing. He is a model train buff and attends model train conventions every year. Similarly, Fran loves Shakespeare and attends the Shakespeare Festival in Stratford, Ontario every summer. They also share vacations together. "We've gotten away from either-or thinking," Fran explains. "We used to take a trip that Larry would want, and the next year one for me. Now we look at the compromises that appeal to both of us, and in the case of our hobbies, if no reasonable compromise exists, we go separately."

Murphy's Law and Surviving with a Sense of Humor

"Jelly bread always falls jelly side down."
—John Gall

Any seasoned traveler will tell you that no matter how many precautions you take, something is bound to go wrong. At one time or another you will find yourself forced to accept accommodations, food, or tickets well above your budget, or of poor quality, or both. You will also face unplanned changes in your schedule. In many of these situations the only reasonable recourse is to grin and bear it. A good sense of humor may be the best survival strategy.

Carol and John have had more than their share of weather and automobile problems while vacationing. "The best is when the canoe fell off the top of the car," she says with a grin. "Also, we got stranded someplace in Ontario during a blizzard, and, of course, the car has broken down several times. But we love to travel and are not going to let little things stop us."

How do Carol and John manage? "We just adapt to the situation at hand," she states. "In many situations, such as the blizzard, we had no choice except to stop. All the highways were closed. We found a motel and decided to make the best of it. Fortunately we had a deck of cards to pass the time."

In their situation, flexibility is critical to vacation pleasure. Carol and John have learned to adapt to various situations and have made it a rule of thumb not to become distressed over unmet deadlines and destinations. It's likely that they will continue to have successful vacations.

Sometimes the problems are less common than bad weather or automobile breakdowns. In our ten years together, Bill and I have faced an array of difficult situations. Once I had my wallet and passport stolen in a London subway station. Another time we waited (with an unhappy baby) for a flight delayed thirty-six hours. Yet another time we arrived in Belgium after all the banks were closed with no local currency and no place to spend the night. (We ended up in the back of a truck.)

While we would never intentionally set up a situation so that problems would be likely to arise, Bill and I travel enough so that we are aware that the unexpected does occur now and then. In our case, creative problem-solving has brought us closer together and helped us appreciate each other more.

Mutual problem-solving can be energizing and promote intimacy. When Bill and I set out for a family reunion in Chicago last summer, we did so with the realization that our baby could be born six weeks early. Because the odds were against it, and because we recognized that we were both fully prepared for a Lamaze birth, we took the risk. When it became clear that we would have the baby in Chicago, we were rapidly faced with many serious decisions. If Bill and I had not been familiar with the childbirth process and the numerous medical interventions available, the experience could have been very frightening. We could have blamed each other for any difficulties which occurred.

As it turned out, we managed to solve the few problems which did arise. Together we were able to make the most prudent decisions and Bill's sense of humor carried me through a long, arduous labor. In the end our short vacation turned out to be a marvelous adventure. All our future trips to Chicago will be colored by the memories of that weekend.

Deciding Not to Go

There may be some instances when after planning a vacation, one of you will have a reason for reconsidering. You owe your partner the respect of listening to the reasons. One of the decision-making methods provided in chapter 1 may be useful if the decision is difficult or not at all clear-cut.

In canceling a vacation you should consider:

1. The emotional impact of the decision on both of you.
2. The opportunity for rescheduling.
3. The possibility of separate vacations.
4. The possibility of retrieving any of the prepaid costs.

Vacations are emotionally laden, and many times one's dreams, fears, sadness, and anger can come to the surface. So when your partner is having misgivings about a vacation, be particularly sensitive to the underlying feelings.

Sometimes canceling a vacation is very practical. I recently canceled a week-long family vacation after recognizing that the stress level in my life was much too high. Instead of rushing off with three small children on a 1,200-mile trip, what I really needed was some time at home, alone, to write and prepare two workshops. For me the trip would have been a hectic routine of crying babies, dirty diapers, and unsterile baby bottles, with my unfinished work gnawing at the back of my mind. I would have come home exhausted to find myself a week behind in my writing and the burden of two workshops ahead of me.

Bill recognized the difficulty of the trip for me and we jointly decided to postpone it until the summer months when my work schedule slows down. My week off was productive and restful—the best "unvacation" I could have had.

Recommended Reading

Brosnahan, Tom. *Frommer's How to Beat the High Cost of Travel.* New York: Simon & Schuster, 1982.

Cross, Wilbur and Farrell Cross. *A Guide to Unusual Vacations.* New York: Hart Publishing Company, 1973.

Cure, Karen. *The Travel Catalogue.* New York: Holt, Rinehart and Winston, 1978.

Eisenberg, Gerson G. *Learning Vacations.* Princeton, New Jersey: Peterson's Guides, 1982.

Shapiro, Stephen A., Ph.D. and Alan J. Tuckman, M.D. *Time Off: A Psychological Guide to Vacations.* Garden City, New York: Anchor Books, 1978.

Woodward, Nancy Hyden. *Vacation!* New York: Penguin Books, 1980.

Footnotes

[1]"PT's Survey Report on How Americans View Vacations." *Psychology Today.* May, 1980, pp. 62–66.

11

Holidays: His Home? Hers? Theirs?

Remember the smell of the Thanksgiving turkey roasting in your grandmother's oven? Or the Christmas when you received your first bicycle? Or opening the door for Elijah at the Passover Seder? For many of us, holidays have a magical quality. They elicit memories of important life events and bring back poignant feelings from childhood.

Holidays are emotionally charged. Sometimes they lift our spirits; occasionally they bring on depression. While many couples report a special intimacy during holidays, others mention a much higher incidence of fighting and ill feelings.

For most of us, holidays achieve the following objectives: (1) they bring us closer to our religious and spiritual selves; (2) they allow us to get in touch with our cultural heritage; (3) they mark passages of time and life; (4) they provide a break from the routine of daily life; and (5) they give us an opportunity to share joyful experiences.

Holidays are problematic, however, because people frequently have different ideas about their importance. Not only are there choices about *which* holidays to celebrate, but also about *how* to celebrate them. While one holiday may have intense religious significance for one person, another person will treat it simply as a day off from work. Others will have certain expectations based on their own childhood and family experiences. No one needs to be told that there is no end to the problems which can arise between a couple deciding on holiday celebrations. It is an area ripe for win-win negotiating.

Which Holidays to Celebrate?

Many couples don't make decisions about which holidays to celebrate, they simply celebrate those that they grew up celebrating. That works out fine except when there are differences in backgrounds.

Jan, for instance, grew up in a New England town where Thanksgiving is the major holiday of the year. It is particularly emphasized in her family whose descendants date back to the Mayflower. Now married to a Californian and living in the Midwest, Jan prefers to return to her parents' home in Connecticut each Thanksgiving for the extended family celebration. Larry, her husband, resisted each year, with the argument that it's just too long a trip for a four-day weekend. Jan felt the long drive was justified for this important celebration. Each year they would fight about it, and each year Jan would insist until Larry gave in. But it was not without hard feelings and resentment from both of them. With this background they decided to negotiate the conflict.

Jan started the discussion by stating that for her the Thanksgiving holiday is one involving both her family and her childhood community. She said that she feels that this holiday is of such immense emotional importance that it symbolizes part of herself—her childhood, her family, her heritage.

Larry who always considered Thanksgiving as a pale precursor of Christmas was surprised at the level of emotion Jan associated with Thanksgiving. Because he felt that Christmas overshadowed Thanksgiving, he unthinkingly assumed that Christmas was the more appropriate holiday to celebrate with Jan's family. Once he recognized the significance of Thanksgiving for Jan, he suggested they brainstorm some options. They started with the premise that Jan would celebrate Thanksgiving with her family. The options included:

1. They would both take extra days off work so they could avoid the holiday traffic on the trip to New England and back.
2. They would take a few days off after Thanksgiving and celebrate both Christmas and Thanksgiving at the end of November.
3. Jan would go to her parents at Thanksgiving even if Larry weren't able to get off work each year.

This kind of agreement was satisfactory to both Jan and Larry. What was critical about it, is that Jan conveyed to Larry the intensity of her desire to spend Thanksgiving with her family in their Connecticut community. Larry now understanding this, willingly worked out solutions to their problem (long drive with holiday traffic over a four-day period) that would allow for her needs and yet reduce the negative parts of the trip for him. Their solutions were win-win in every respect.

Jan and Larry's conflict was solved by bettering their communication. Once Jan communicated to Larry the intensity of her desire to spend Thanksgiving at her childhood home, they were able to work out some solutions.

Not all holiday conflicts can be resolved by improving communications, however. Take Bonnie and Jeff. Bonnie grew up in a family where Christmas was the major holiday and family event of the year. Jeff is Jewish. Neither is particularly religious, and, in fact, they have found very few differences in their ethics and choice of lifestyle. But they do have a problem at Christmas. Bonnie wants to celebrate it and Jeff doesn't. States Bonnie, "I've explained to Jeff it's not a religious thing to me—just a cultural one. I grew up with the joy and wonderment of Christmas and I want to continue it. I'm more than willing to celebrate the Jewish holidays also, but Jeff wants no part of that either."

Jeff counters Bonnie's statement by saying, "When we got married we decided not to make religion an issue. Since we are both non-religious, we should simply skip the holidays."

Jeff and Bonnie face a conflict in cultural values. For Jeff the religious holidays (albeit secularized) hold little value. Bonnie views them differently and wants to maintain Christmas as a part of her life which holds much pleasure.

In this situation Jeff might do well to recognize Bonnie's real intent here— to recognize an event that was a significant part of her life for many years. Since she is willing to reciprocate, he should not feel threatened.

Bonnie feels like she is at an impasse. What can she do in a negotiation session? The following are some suggestions:

1. *Ease into it.* Suggest a simple gift exchange the first year with a Christmas tree the following year. Allow Jeff the time to get used to a small observance of Christmas which he can enjoy.
2. *Combine Hanukkah and Christmas* to make an "ecumenical" holiday. Both light candles and hang wreaths.
3. *Celebrate with other couples of mixed backgrounds.* How have they resolved these issues? Borrow ideas from them.

While Jeff may not welcome any of these suggestions, they do provide a starting point for an honest discussion. Because this is such an important issue for Bonnie, Jeff would be well-advised to consider some sort of compromise or trade-off so he can feel that he is gaining as well as giving.

In the end it's important to recognize those holidays that are important to your partner and understand *why* they are important. Once you get to that point it's much easier to drive to Connecticut or decorate a Christmas tree. It's a matter of recognizing your partner's individuality and heritage and being willing to affirm it with understanding and love.

With Whom to Spend Holidays?

The choice of whom to visit on the holidays may be even more difficult than deciding which holidays to celebrate. The choice of friends versus family or immediate family versus extended family can be stressful. This stress is accentuated when family members have rigid ideas about what is appropriate and inappropriate for certain holidays.

Even if you and your partner are in complete agreement over your choice of companions for a particular holiday, you may find yourself defending your decision with parents, grandparents, or other relatives. It may not be easy to face Aunt Maude who has said she's going to make your favorite pecan pies, "even though you can't take a few minutes to stop by the house." Or, your whole family may be meeting at the summer cottage on Labor Day, and you will be the only member absent—the first time in ten years that anyone has missed this event. Guilt, guilt, guilt!

In situations where you and your partner choose separate plans over those of the extended family, it is important to weigh the consequences of making this split from the family. Some questions to consider include:

1. Will a serious rift result if you don't attend the family gathering? If so, how will you be able to mend it—if at all? What length of time will be needed for the ill feelings to pass?
2. If you choose not to attend will you be able to enjoy yourself knowing that the family is having a gathering elsewhere? Will you be able to handle the guilt and let it pass?
3. On the other hand, will your actions be looked on favorably by other family members who would also prefer a different activity? Will you be breaking ground and giving others more freedom in the future? Will they give you emotional support for your decision?
4. If you choose to attend the family event, what can you do to make the best of the situation? What can your partner do to help and support you?
5. If you choose not to attend the event, what can your partner do to help and support you?

The choice of whom you'll spend the holidays with is acutely sensitive. Ed and Tricia are a case in point. When I asked Tricia about their Christmas plans, she went into a tirade. "I never have a good time at Christmas. It's just awful. Because I try not to hurt people's feelings, we end up making three or four stops to see my relatives on Christmas Day. Besides that, Ed wants to stay home with the baby. And I'd like to do that, too. My relatives would be angry and hurt if I didn't go to see them, and Ed is if I do. By the end of Christmas Day I always have a headache."

Tricia has put herself into a bind. By driving all over town on Christmas Day in order to placate her relatives, she is ruining the holiday for both herself and Ed. She readily admits that she doesn't like the current practice; the pace is much too hectic. Tricia would welcome a change, but is afraid to hurt her relatives.

What can she and Ed do? Some alternatives come to mind.

1. Visit the relatives on another day. Or spread their visits over several days.
2. Ask the relatives to visit Tricia and Ed at home either on Christmas, or, preferably, on another day.
3. Explain to the relatives the dizzying pace of the visits and give them each a phone call instead of a visit.

While these solutions (and there are no doubt others) are simple, they are admittedly very difficult to implement. Family traditions die hard and are very emotionally laden. *It is not easy to break a tradition without feeling a sense of loss or a sense of guilt.* You need to be prepared to deal with that sense of loss and guilt when making such changes.

One effective method of dealing with these feelings is to support each other after you have made your decision. Tricia, undoubtedly, will need to have Ed encourage her and tell her how much better it is to stay home on Christmas, rather than driving all over town. In making the change, they should focus on activities that will make the day meaningful for themselves as a couple.

Similarly, you may want to seek support from friends and relatives who have faced similar situations. Ask them how they felt when they made the change. How did they deal with the guilt? Or with irate relatives? What hints do they have to offer?

Frequently there is no clear-cut method for dealing with family events— particularly if they are a long distance away. A trip from Chicago to Houston cannot be compromised as easily as a Sunday picnic only five miles from home. In making the decision to attend a family event, you may choose to write out a pro and con list or use a decision-making grid to weigh the priorities. Table 11.1 illustrates the pro and con list for a couple who are deciding whether to visit relatives at Passover.

Table 11.1

Sally and Richard's Pro and Con List
Shall We Visit Richard's Family at Passover?

Pro	Con
1. We haven't seen them for a year.	1. There are likely to be bitter remarks and several fights between Richard and his sisters.
2. Richard's father is in ill health and may not recover.	2. The cost for the whole family to fly out is considerable.
3. Richard's parents would love to see the children.	3. The house will be cramped.

The Decision: After discussing each of the points on their pro and con list, Sally and Richard decided to make the trip. The decision was based on the following: (1) They wanted Richard's parents to be able to see the children; it had been almost a year and the kids had grown a lot. (2) Richard would make an extra effort not to fight with his sisters. Sally agreed to wink at Richard as a signal to cool down if he seemed to be getting angry. (3) They would try to book a supersaver to cut the cost of the flight. (4) They would stay at a motel despite the extra cost. That way they could get away when tension was mounting and the small house wouldn't seem so claustrophobic.

In situations where you and your partner are at odds, you will need to use even more sophisticated negotiation skills. If you become deadlocked with your partner over a particular holiday, you may need to consider celebrating it separately or compromise and alternate from year to year. Or you may need to set aside a second day to celebrate the same holiday. In working out your decision you will need to take into consideration the strengths of your partner's desires as well as your own. You will also need to consider your willingness to compromise.

Cheryl and Allen chose to spend Christmas separately with their respective out-of-town families while they were living together. After they were married, however, they alternated Christmases, spending one with her parents and the next with his. This arrangement worked well until the birth of their daughter. Then they chose to remain in their own home and invited the grandparents to come and visit for the holidays.

Cheryl comments, "Our Christmas celebrations have progressed parallel with our relationship. At first we viewed ourselves as separate individuals and 'home' was still our parents' houses. However, over the years and especially after starting our own family, 'home' is right here with us. Allen and I both want Santa to come down our chimney, not that of either of our parents."

Also faced with two sets of parents and one Christmas, Diane and Burt have worked out a different arrangement for celebrating the Christmas holidays. They celebrate Christmas Eve and morning at home with their two sons. Diane's family lives nearby, so they attend a large family gathering with them on Christmas evening. A week later, they drive five hours to visit Ed's family for another "Christmas" over the New Year's holiday. Both Diane and Ed are happy with the arrangement in that it spreads out the holidays. "It's the best of all worlds," Diane states. "We get to spend Christmas at home and are still able to enjoy the holidays with both families."

Sometimes the arrangements are not so easily compromised. Stacy and Jack are both remarried with children from each previous marriage as well as having a new baby together. They must deal with two ex-spouses and their respective two new spouses in addition to eight sets of grandparents! In working out the logistics of this complicated situation, they must take into consideration geographical distance, emotional closeness, and their own stamina. While there are no easy answers, Stacy and Jack have found that maintaining a sense of humor helps them make it through Christmas, birthdays, and other holidays. They, however, are currently considering abandoning everyone and taking off to a desert island for the next three years.

Traditions

Holidays are fraught with traditions. Traditions can be centuries old or they can be established in one year. They range from the simple to the sublime—an orange in the toe of a Christmas stocking to the Mormon Tabernacle Choir singing the "Hallelujah Chorus." Traditions provide structure to holidays. They also elicit memories of bygone years.

Traditions can be serious, frivolous, or simply caloric. One family I know reads the biblical Christmas story every Christmas Eve. They also "pig out" on a wonderful assortment of Christmas breads and pastries the next morning. Both traditions are important to this family which has chosen to continue them faithfully year after year.

Negotiating Traditions

Maintaining Family Traditions. You may find yourselves negotiating conflicts over whose traditions to maintain. Some families open Christmas presents on Christmas Eve; others open them on Christmas morning. Some families have lamb for the Passover Seder; others have turkey. Some families have a large Easter breakfast, others have Easter dinner.

In these situations you will have to be sensitive to both the practical and the emotional issues involved. In my family only the children had Christmas stockings. Adults exchanged wrapped gifts. But Bill insists on getting a Christmas stocking each year. It's certainly not necessary, or for that matter, very practical, because most of the gifts I give him are too large to fit in his stocking. But it's an emotional issue for Bill, so as a concession to him we have Christmas stockings as well as a gift exchange.

When negotiating traditions with your partner be sure to consider the intensity of each of your feelings. If you both have strong feelings, is there a way to incorporate both traditions into your holidays? Can you open half of the presents on Christmas Eve and half on Christmas morning? Or can you switch from year to year. Lamb this year, turkey next year? Chances are you may grow to enjoy some of your partner's traditions and begin to view them as your own.

Establishing Your Own New Traditions. I have found that couples with good, solid, long-lasting relationships have established many of their own traditions associated with holidays and special days. The traditions range from routine activities such as carving Jack-O-Lanterns to more serious matters such as renewing their marriage vows every year.

Frequently a change in lifestyle sets a pattern for starting a new tradition. You move into your own home, so you decide to spend Christmas there. You start a garden, and from then on you do your planting on Memorial Day. Or your new boat spurs you to spend the Fourth of July and Labor Day on the water and soon it's a full-fledged tradition.

Others consciously start a new tradition with their own families. In an effort to separate the religious from the secular during Christmas season, Christine and Bob started a St. Nicholas Day tradition on December 6. On St. Nicholas Eve the children put out their shoes for St. Nicholas. In the morning they find the shoes filled with snacks and toys for each child. After the family has enjoyed the gifts from St. Nicholas, the family has a special breakfast together. "This tradition marks the beginning of the holiday season for us," states Bob. "It allows us a special time with the children, and we have more time at Christmas to focus on the religious aspects of the holiday."

In establishing your own traditions, such as Bob and Christine did, you are, in essence, demonstrating that your own special days should be recognized. Each partner agrees that these special events have enough meaning to warrant celebrating them again and again, year after year.

Several ways to celebrate the various holidays are suggested in books listed in the Recommended Reading section at the end of this chapter. Many are old, established traditions. Others offer new approaches. You may want to sit down with your partner and decide which kinds of celebrations and traditions provide the most meaning and pleasure for you—both as individuals and as a couple.

Eliminating Traditions. Many holiday practices no longer make sense in today's world. Because of logistics some traditions cannot be maintained. Children may live long distances from their families and not be able to participate in family celebrations. Or our lifestyles don't permit the time. Or the old traditions no longer have meaning.

As a full-time working mother I have had to eliminate some traditions which are simply impractical. One is my family's custom of making our Christmas gifts. Not being artistically inclined anyway, I found this practice an impossibility with a full-time job, a part-time consulting business, and three young children. After giving up the burden of making several gifts each year, I have found that the Christmas season is much more pleasant and relaxed.

Similarly, some traditions out of necessity have been modified. Sylvia and Herb have come to love and expect to make Christmas cookies every year with their children. They enjoy using cookie cutters and creating fancy designs with the icing. In recent years they have continued to make Christmas cookies, but have used ready-made dough and tube frosting. This cuts out at least an hour from the preparation time and the whole family enjoys the process.

Your lifestyle may very well dictate that you give up some traditions— perhaps only temporarily. One year when Bill was serving a demanding internship at an out-of-town psychiatric hospital and I was working full time plus taking graduate courses, we simply chose not to take part in some of our routine Christmas activities. For instance, we gave away our tickets to the *Messiah* and *Nutcracker Suite* and put up our Christmas tree on Christmas Eve—an activity we ordinarily would do two or three weeks before Christmas. While we did miss the activities that year, I found the extra time allowed us to maintain a balance in the other critical areas of life. Table 11.2 provides some suggestions for practices you may choose to eliminate for matters of time or practicality.

Table 11.2

Holiday Practices You May Want to Eliminate

Elaborate Multi-Course Meals. It may be easier and actually better for family harmony to have an elegant meal at a restaurant or an informal meal at home than to labor hours for one meal.

Exhausting Drives. Have you ever knocked yourself out in order to make it to a certain event on time, only to find yourself too tired to enjoy the occasion? Either arrange to start the trip earlier or postpone the celebration until later.

Overspending. You've heard this one before. Your children, parents, and friends will not love you any more if you overspend your budget.

Rigid Rules. It may be too much to ask small children to wait until after a meal to open gifts. Perhaps if they are allowed to open one present before the meal, the meal itself will be more pleasant. Similarly, teenagers might be given a choice in holiday activities rather than being coerced to attend certain ones. Adults, too, need to recognize that "the way we've always done it" may not be appropriate any given year.

Televised Sports. Frequently some members of a family will use televised sports as a barrier to communicating with family members on important holidays.

Unhealthy Foods. While it is certainly fine to have sweets on special occasions, perhaps you don't need pumpkin pie, apple pie, mincemeat pie, *and* ice cream all on your Thanksgiving menu. And if you can't possibly eliminate any single item, you needn't feel obligated to eat the leftovers for the following three weeks.

Traditions should reflect our growth and change. However, because they tend to be maintained year after year without regard to the changes in lifestyle, they frequently become cumbersome or lose their meaning. We may need to alter some of them to reflect our growth. Just as a couple may celebrate Christmas at home once the baby is born, so might we need to establish other practices more compatible with our lifestyles—perhaps a drink-free New Year's Eve or a Fourth of July without firecrackers. Holidays, after all, are for people and by people. If you're a vegetarian, you do not skip Thanksgiving, but instead you celebrate with a delicious and carefully prepared feast where the absence of meat is not given a moment's notice. After all, it's not the turkey, but the joy and closeness of the people you're with that hold the holidays together. As win-win negotiators we need to recognize this and create situations conducive to strengthening family ties and friendships.

Difficult Holidays

Religious Holidays

Respect is a key ingredient of a good relationship and is of primary importance when two people have differing religious beliefs. It is not critical that you hold the same religious beliefs as your partner, but you must allow your partner that freedom.

Interestingly enough, many couples who come from the same religious background have divergent views about religious holidays. For example, Sue and Chuck were raised in the same religious faith and hold very similar beliefs. However, they disagree pointedly about how to celebrate Easter. She wants the family to attend religious services throughout the Holy Week culminating with a sunrise service on Easter morning—just as her family did. Chuck's focus, however, is on the family and the more secularized aspects of the holiday. He wants to sleep in on Easter morning and then have an Easter egg hunt followed by a big family breakfast—just like his family used to do.

Similarly, Marilyn and Jerry have difficulty deciding on the celebration of Hanukkah. They have two children and Jerry likes to celebrate the holidays by giving them lavish gifts. He also enjoys the candle-lighting ceremony every evening. Marilyn, on the other hand, views this kind of celebration as a "mock Christmas" and would rather cut down on the gifts and observe Hanukkah as what she contends it really is, a "minor holiday."

In these cases negotiation skills are critical. Both couples will need to have serious discussions and come up with solutions which meet the needs of each individual without compromising their faith. It's also important to be sensitive to your partner's religion. If it's extremely important to your partner that you attend a particular religious service, it certainly makes sense to consider doing so. While you youself may not feel the need to attend, you show respect to your partner by going along. It's necessary to communicate very clearly with your partner and find out exactly his or her expectations and desires. The worst that is likely to happen is that you will be bored sitting through some unintelligible Hebrew or Latin. At best you may gain a better understanding of your partner.

Your negotiation skills may be useful if you or your partner choose to commit a large amount of time to religious services or activities. You will both need to take a look at what each of you considers an appropriate amount of time and compromise, if necessary.

Similarly, you may need to compromise on which holidays to celebrate. Judy and Dan, coming from Protestant and Jewish backgrounds, have an agreement to celebrate Christmas, Easter, and Passover at home with the children. But they also attend Rosh Hashanah and Yom Kippur services each fall. Linda also attends B'hai events with her husband John although she is not a B'hai herself. Evan and Marie alternate going to their respective churches each Sunday. However you work it out, it is important to have respect for your partner and work out an arrangement that suits both of you.

The Christmas Season

The Christmas season, without a doubt, generates more anxiety than any other holiday period. Interestingly, non-Christians as well as Christians report that they frequently have difficulty coping with this time of year. There are a number of reasons why this season poses so many problems for so many people.

1. *It is an emotional time.* Memories of childhood experiences emerge. Frequently adults make elaborate attempts to relive the Christmases of their youth or to recreate the perfect Christmas that they never had.

2. *It is all-pervasive.* Streets, stores, restaurants, offices, and private homes are decorated with ubiquitous reminders of the holidays. Even the most casual conversations often touch on holiday plans, shopping, and the hustle-bustle of Christmas activities. It's just about impossible to go anywhere or talk to anyone without some reminder of the Christmas season.

3. *There is an emphasis on family, particularly the extended family during this time of year.* For many this involves relationships which may be strained. It also creates stress for people in different family situations— particularly for those recently separated or divorced, or who have experienced the death of a loved one. Couples who have chosen not to have children may feel increased pressure from relatives at this time of year. For couples whose children have left home, there may be a feeling of emptiness or increased nostalgia for bygone holidays.

4. *The obligation of gift-giving.* Many people find the chores associated with purchasing and wrapping gifts so overwhelming that it clouds the entire holiday season. Others procrastinate and never finish the shopping. Or once they do finish, they decide that what they have chosen isn't enough, so they take on the burden (and the expense) all over again until Christmas arrives.

5. *The "shoulds" of tradition.* Many people get caught up in the obligation of sending Christmas cards to too many people. Others labor for hours making dozens of Christmas cookies because it has become a part of their tradition. Still others, every year, take on the burden of the office party or the extended family dinner.

6. *The Christmas season is lengthy.* For most people it extends from four to eight weeks, a significant amount of time.

Coping Strategies for the Christmas Season

If you or your partner have difficulty coping with the Christmas season, it would be wise to discuss the problems well in advance of the season. August wouldn't be too early. If one or both of you has difficulty sorting out what you really want from the vast array of activities available, Table 11.3, the Christmas and Hanukkah Priority Checklist, may be of help.

Table 11.3

Christmas and Hanukkah Priority Checklist

Both you and your partner should rank your priorities individually. Use 1 for most important and 13 for least important. After you have both separately completed the ordering, compare your lists. Which priorities are high on both lists? Which are low on both lists? Which are in conflict? You will need to negotiate the ones in conflict.

Nuclear Family Time. Spending time with my immediate family. These family members include _____.

Extended Family Time. Spending time with my extended family. These family members include _____.

Religious Emphasis. Attending special services, ceremonies, midnight Mass, cantatas.

Gift Exchange. With family and friends.

Santa Claus. Being Santa to the kids and sharing their delight on Christmas morning.

Parties and Entertaining. Attending and hosting parties during the holiday season. Enjoying the festivities with colleagues and friends.

Helping the Needy. By volunteering help or by making donations to charities.

Decorating. Spending time decorating the house and making a special effort to create a festive environment.

Entertainment. Attending movies, sports events, concerts, or plays. Going caroling or listening to holiday music at home.

Holiday Cooking. Making and/or consuming favorite recipes.

Expressing My Creativity. Through homemade gifts, decorations, cards, or art.

Time to Relax. A break from work to stay at home and unwind.

Time to Travel. A few days off to go away and explore new places.

From there outline your fantasy of a pleasant and meaningful holiday season. Detail any activities that are important to you. Which activities do you want your partner to share? Which activities could you enjoy without your partner? Be prepared to discuss and negotiate these with your partner. Once you have finalized your holiday plans, put them on a joint calendar and post it in a prominent place, such as a refrigerator or cupboard door.

Table 11.4, Irene and Jay's Christmas List, illustrates this method with each of them listing their own priorities. Although at first glance their priorities seemed far apart, they were able to work them out. When Irene and Jay started to discuss their desires for the holiday season, they recognized that their main conflict was over free time and structured time. They resolved the situation by Jay agreeing to participate in the activities on Irene's list, but to leave the rest of the holiday period free for rest and relaxation. Irene agreed to get together with her relatives on the Sunday after Christmas, rather than on Christmas Day. They agreed to ask the children for their priorities regarding sledding, skating, games, and parties.

Table 11.4
Irene and Jay's Christmas List

Irene	Jay
1. Spend Christmas morning alone with the family to exchange gifts.	1. Time to relax.
2. Get together with my family for a large meal and gift exchange on Christmas Day.	2. Christmas day at home with just the children, no relatives.
3. Attend Christmas Eve Mass.	3. Time to play games with the children.
4. Go to the kids' Christmas concert.	4. Fewer structured activities and more free time.
5. Make cookies.	
6. Go to the *Messiah*.	
7. Decorate the tree with the whole family.	
8. Take the children sledding and ice skating.	
9. Go to the neighbors' annual party.	
10. Go to the New Year's party at the Smiths'.	

Frequently a couple may need to consider not only what they want during the holiday season, but also what they want to avoid. Table 11.5, Jane and Mike's "I Don't Want" Christmas List, illustrates how each of them listed unpleasant situations they wished to avoid during the Christmas season.

Table 11.5

Jane and Mike's "I Don't Want" Christmas List

Jane's List	Mike's List
I don't want to do any last minute shopping the week before Christmas.	I don't want Jane to complain that she's too tired to enjoy the holidays.
I don't want to cook a big meal on Christmas day.	I don't want to put together any toys, bikes, wagons, or other gifts on Christmas Eve.
I don't want to stay late at Mike's office party.	I don't want to have to apologize to Jane for getting the wrong size or color or style of gift again this year.
I don't want the television on at all on Christmas Eve or Christmas Day.	

Interestingly, both Jane and Mike were surprised at how few "I don't wants" they each had, particularly because the holiday season is exceedingly stressful for both of them. In working out a solution, they both agreed to follow each other's list with the following provisions:

1. They would buy delicatessen trays and snacks for Christmas Day rather than cook a big turkey dinner.
2. They would assemble the Christmas toys and bicycles on the Sunday preceding Christmas.
3. Jane would give Mike a list with exactly what she wanted for Christmas, including sizes, colors, and even stores where the items were available. Jane agreed to list a lot of items so that Mike would have no difficulty finding them and she could still be surprised.
4. They would leave Mike's office party by 11:00 P.M.
5. Mike would do any unexpected last minute shopping that came up the week before Christmas.
6. Jane would not complain as long as she didn't have any last minute shopping or a big Christmas dinner to cook.
7. There would be no television on Christmas Eve or Christmas Day.
8. Mike would do all the gift refunds and exchanges which were necessary.

They posted a list on the bathroom mirror and reminded each other whenever any of the items came up. Mike was delighted with Jane's change in attitude. Her complaints were few and she enjoyed the holidays much more. Jane agreed that by being relieved of many burdens she could relax and savor the holidays.

While Christmas is the holiday that poses the greatest number of problems for the greatest number of people, it is by no means unique. The problems and solutions suggested in this section can be applied to Passover or Independence Day or anniversaries. Win-win negotiating has no bounds, it will work for Rosh Hashanah, the Chinese New Year, the B'hai New Year, January first, or—if you wish—all four.

Other Holiday Obligations

Frequently the pressures of gift giving and entertaining spoil the holidays. It's simply too hectic with the pressures of shopping, gift wrapping, food preparation, and housecleaning. How do you get all these obligations out of the way and allow yourself to enjoy the holidays?

First, take some tips from the time-management experts. These include:
1. Make a "to do" list and prioritize it.
2. Eliminate all unnecessary items from the list.
3. Put deadlines after each item.
4. If a task is too overwhelming, divide it into smaller components and then add deadlines.
5. Put all deadlines on your calendar and utilize your calendar daily.
6. Delegate the work as much as possible.

Entertaining

Entertaining can be very time consuming and energy draining. If you need to entertain in a formal manner for professional reasons, consider hiring a caterer and professional cleaning service. If not, then entertain with an informal arrangement such as a pot luck, pizza and beer, or dessert only. After all, the food is just an excuse for enjoying one another's company, isn't it?

Table 11.6 provides a checklist for Helen and Tom's annual open house. Fifty to sixty adults and twenty to thirty children attend this annual event and just about everyone seems to have a good time. Amazingly, Helen and Tom have pared down the preparation time to about four hours spread over the course of a month.

Because the open house is at the peak of the holiday season, the arrangements could very well be cumbersome. However, the couple has utilized various time-management techniques so that each year the party gets larger but the preparation gets easier. They indicate on the invitations that it is an informal pot-luck, and they supply the traditional black-eyed peas and buttermilk, a Southern custom from Tom's childhood. They also indicate on the invitation that children are welcome, so that the guests have no doubts about whether to bring them along and there are no last minute phone calls or inquiries.

Table 11.6

Helen and Tom's Preparation Checklist for a Fast, Easy, and Incredibly Successful New Year's Day Open House

Time Spent	Activity	Date
30 minutes	Write up invitations and take to print shop.	December 1
30 minutes	Pick up invitations and purchase stamps.	December 7
1 hour	Address, stamp, and mail invitations.	December 10
1 hour	Purchase groceries and liquor.	December 27
30 minutes	Prepare black-eyed peas.	December 31
30 minutes	Set up dishes, food, liquor, trash bins, games, and chairs. Have children straighten up house.	January 1

The key to successful entertaining lies in your attitude. If you provide an environment which is comfortable and pleasant, chances are that your guests will respond positively. Helen and Tom could choose to get uptight about their gigantic party, but their casual approach rubs off on the guests. They are free to relax and enjoy themselves. If something goes wrong—a child spills his plate or the beer supply runs out—it's no big deal, someone will clean up the mess and someone will run out for more beer. The party goes on.

Gift Purchasing

Gift purchasing also can be made easier using time-management techniques. The following are some tips to make gift obligations easier.

1. Always start with a list. If you have no ideas, then ask each person for a gift suggestion list.
2. Have the gift wrapped at the store or keep a well-stocked supply of paper, ribbons, and cards at home at all times.
3. Purchase packages for out-of-town deliveries at stores which will mail them for you. Most department stores, bookstores, and record shops will do this for a minimum fee or at no extra charge beyond postage.
4. Use the phone, not your feet, to see which stores have a particular item.
5. Don't wait to buy the perfect gift or to find the best price if the event is within two weeks. Perfection requires a big head start. However, do keep receipts and tags so that items may be exchanged.
6. If you have children, keep a supply of birthday gifts along with gift-

wrapping supplies on hand so that a late invitation doesn't wreak havoc with your schedule.

7. Buy duplicate gifts during the Christmas season for people such as childcare workers, housecleaners, and co-workers. Give plants one year, a favorite liquor another, and mixed nuts another year. This way you can purchase all the gifts at once and you won't forget from year to year what you've already given.

8. Buy the same gift each year. Each Christmas our son's elementary teacher receives notecards; our newspaper carrier receives chocolate candy. Usually these are different people each year, but I doubt if they would mind the duplicate gifts if they happened to receive them two years in a row.

Birthdays and Anniversaries

During our work with individuals and couples in therapy, Bill and I have noticed that people having difficulty with self-esteem frequently choose not to celebrate their birthdays. Similarly, couples experiencing difficulty in their relationship frequently ignore their wedding anniversaries. This practice is emotionally unhealthy. At the very least it magnifies a poor self-image and discourages an optimistic attitude about the growth of the relationship. And besides, birthdays and anniversaries can be fun-filled, joyous occasions.

Birthdays. Celebrating your birthday is affirming your existence. It is a time to enjoy yourself and separate yourself from your various roles, to get away from being a parent or a worker or a nurturing spouse, and for a few hours do exactly what you want to do. On your birthday you're in the spotlight—the center of attention. It's a good time to get in touch with the "kid" inside you. That may mean having a party with special friends and getting lots of presents, having cake and ice cream with your family, or doing something special like going to an amusement park or a special play or concert.

If you can't figure out how to get in touch with the playful, childlike part of yourself, try observing small children when they celebrate their own birthdays. They will be excited, silly, and very demanding. They also will know exactly what they want and be very imaginative. Capturing this child within you will likely have a positive effect on your partner as well. Happy, joyful people are fun to be around—on birthdays or any other day.

If you wrack your brain and are still having trouble coming up with birthday party ideas, consider the following:

1. checking into a local luxury hotel for an evening or weekend,
2. getting a professional massage, manicure or pedicure,
3. going bicycling or canoeing,
4. organizing a hayride or sleighride party, or
5. renting an X-rated movie.

Anniversaries. Anniversaries are special dates in a couple's relationship. We generally think of wedding anniversaries, but other important dates can be celebrated:

1. your first meeting,
2. your first date,
3. your first lovemaking, or
4. your first day of living together.

The possibilities go on and on, but the point is that relationships need affirmation. Anniversaries allow us to reflect on the past and the situations we have faced together. They also allow us to look toward the future—both as individuals and as a couple. And most important, anniversaries allow us the opportunity to share in the joy of the moment, to delight in the union of two people who have weathered crises, survived, and thrived.

One of the best things you can do to affirm your relationship is celebrate your togetherness. Depending on your personalities and lifestyle, you may choose to do this in a variety of ways. Dinner out at an elegant restaurant is a frequent choice. Some couples choose to take a weekend trip away. Still others take more offbeat approaches like renting billboards or skywriters to proclaim their love for one another. Whatever you choose, use your anniversary to renew your relationship and add joy to your life.

Beginnings and Endings

When it comes down to it, holidays provide us with the opportunity to acknowledge life's changes. You get married and suddenly you have another family. You have a baby and your family treats you differently. Your children grow up and become adults and you develop new relationships with them. Some of the changes are rough; some you welcome with open arms.

Of course, not all of the changes we encounter warrant joyful celebrations. Deaths and tragic events will touch our lives, and their anniversary dates will haunt us from year to year. Psychologically it is important to acknowledge these days. The acknowledgment itself is part of the mourning and subsequent healing process.

On these dark days it is only natural to reflect on the past and look for strength in the promise of the future. While holidays and anniversaries remind us of the cycles in life, they also teach us that life is fleeting. A simple holiday ornament or tradition passed from generation to generation may remind us, as it did our parents and grandparents, that we are mortal. And that mortality allows us to cherish life even more.

Recommended Reading

Chambers, Wicke and Spring Asher. *The Celebration Book of Great American Traditions.* New York: Harper & Row, 1983.

Del Re, Gerard and Patricia. *The Christmas Almanack.* Garden City, New York: Doubleday & Co., 1979.

Gregory, Ruth W. *Anniversaries and Holidays.* Chicago: American Library Association, 1975.

Myers, Robert J. *Celebrations: The Complete Book of American Holidays.* Garden City, New York: Doubleday & Co., 1972.

Shannon-Thornberry, Milo. *The Alternate Celebrations Catalogue.* New York: The Pilgrim Press, 1982.

12

Playtime: The Joint
(or Disjointed) Pursuit of Leisure

Up in the air. No, it's not superman. It's Jack, your next door neighbor, hang-gliding. Or Jane, your secretary, ballooning. Or Jill, your accountant, in her ultra-light.

Leisure is a valuable commodity of modern life. Americans put a great premium on leisure and the wide variety of activities made available through a combination of spare time and money. Measured in economic terms, leisure is a growth industry. In the past decade the amount of money spent on leisure has more than doubled. Currently 5 percent of the American household budget is spent directly on leisure products and services.[1]

The scope of leisure time is also significant. Generally speaking, the national average is about thirty-five hours per week—more for younger and older people and less for those employed full-time. This is time apart from work and chores. It is discretionary time, time to indulge in any number of activities currently available—from birdwatching to deep-sea diving to reading a Robert Parker mystery.

Leisure choices are critical to the well-being of most relationships. Issues such as how much time to spend together on joint activities versus time for individual pursuits frequently need to be negotiated. Often couples have different expectations, not only for the amount of joint time to allocate, but also how to use that time. Family and work obligations, television, and individual hobbies can also be a source of conflict. Like so many other areas, leisure time is a topic easily adapted to the process of win-win negotiating.

Leisure and New Values

As the baby boomers have grown into adulthood, they have brought with them a new set of values that focus squarely on leisure. Play has become as important, or in some cases, more important than work. People have begun to define themselves by their leisure time activities—sometimes even over their occupations. In the book *Great Expectations,* which explores the effect the baby-boom generation is having on society, author Landon Y. Jones states that since "only 20 percent of people say that work means more to them than pleasure, the answer to the old question, What do you do? is not as interesting as asking, How do you play?"[2]

This new type of self-definition results in many people viewing themselves primarily through their leisure pursuits as joggers or model train buffs or baseball card collectors. Their professional occupations become secondary to their non-work activities. For many people a job is simply a means of producing income to support their hobbies. You've met such people. John works as an insurance agent but his real love is horses. Andrea works as a secretary but the biggest interest in her life is sailing.

Frequently such non-work activities become as overwhelming and time-consuming as the traditional "organization man's" career. For example, marathon running requires a tremendous commitment of time and self-discipline for several months before the event. As the marathon date approaches, the runner becomes more and more obsessed with the event, giving attention to many details of proper training. While the runner will continue with other life activities, the marathon is always at the back of his or her mind.

To understand these changing values Daniel Yankelovich, a pollster and leading analyst of social change, surveyed thousands of young Americans. What he found, not surprisingly, is that baby boomers were brought up with the idea of achieving the American Dream. They expected to go to college, then to go on to obtain interesting and high-paying jobs, and then quickly to surpass their parents' standard of living. However, for most this dream has not been realized. Once the baby boomers started entering the work force, they began to face stiff competition for the few jobs available. States Jones:

> Each time the boom generation climbed into an older age group, the unemployment rate shot up in that age group while its earning power declined. The difficulties were made all the harder to bear because the boom generation's lengthy education had nurtured such high expectations. Eventually one of the prime articles of faith in the American credo— that a college education will pay off—was undermined. That was not the worst of it. Economists were concluding that competitive stresses that had marked the baby boom's early years could only become stronger. Forever

shackled to the oversupply inherent in its large numbers, the boom generation would be doomed to a life of low earnings, career disappointments, and personal struggle.[3]

Facing this kind of labor market, it is not surprising that young people have sought new ways of defining themselves. Play, with its many competitive elements, conveniently serves this purpose.

Although they are professionals who do have a good earning capability, John and Cindy reflect these new values. John, a computer specialist with an MBA states, "Jobs are just not that important to us. They're a source of income to support the lifestyle we've chosen." Cindy, a former physical therapist, now chooses to stay home with their two children. John and Cindy focus their lives on their family, friends, and leisure. They go square dancing three or four times a week—their most active interest at present. They also take pride in their backyard garden and indoor light garden. They spend much time with their children and a large circle of friends.

John and Cindy are typical baby boomers with a new set of work values and attitudes toward leisure. Both are bright, well-educated, and have worked in demanding, professional positions. But both indicate their current focus is on their non-work time—they gain their primary identities from these activities, not their careers.

Given this preoccupation with leisure pursuits by a whole new generation of young adults, it is not surprising that many couples have difficulty deciding what to do with their leisure. If the decision involves self-definition for one or both partners it is necessarily serious and complicated.

Even individuals who have less ego involvement with their leisure pursuits face numerous choices. Shall I pursue one large or several lesser activities? Shall I include my partner? Does my partner want me involved in his or her leisure activities? How do we go about scheduling all of this?

We or Me? Joint Versus Individual Time

She's been waiting two hours for him to finish a computer program so that they can go to the beach. He's had to rush through the program because he hasn't had a large enough block of uninterrupted time to finish it properly. Both are on edge and angry with each other.

Sound familiar? Frequently couples are unaware, at least on a conscious level, of their need to openly negotiate joint and individual time. Somehow they expect each other's time needs to be the same, even if their interests aren't.

Time, like any other commodity, often needs to be discussed and negotiated, with compromises if necessary. How you decide to split your time will depend on several variables: (1) how you both spend your working hours;

(2) whether you have children; (3) whether you share similar interests and favorite forms of entertainment; (4) whether you participate in the same sports and aerobic activities; (5) whether you both have your own circle of individual friends as well as joint friends; (6) whether you have a single interest that occupies a large amount of time.

Because this can become overwhelming, I recommend approaching the subject in this way: decide on weekly joint activities, schedule them, and leave the rest of the time for individual pursuits. Then during some of your individual time you can invite your partner to join you in an activity. He or she then has the option of joining you or not.

For example, Judy and Alan have standing dates with each other every Friday and Saturday evening. They also save Sunday and Wednesday nights for time together at home. Alan says, "It usually turns out that we have other weeknights together, but we save these two as a guarantee. Sometimes when demands get heavy we trade our Wednesday night at home for another night, but usually we're both able to keep it open."

Alan and Judy's approach gives them guaranteed time together—both for going out and for staying home. They are pleased with the arrangement, in that it gives them both sufficient time for their individual interests as well. They can pursue their hobbies without feeling guilty or concerned that they're not spending enough time with each other.

Similarly Marcia and Jeff play paddleball every Friday night. They also spend Saturday nights together, but leave the activity open for discussion from weekend to weekend. They also stay home together every Sunday evening. Marcia states, "Sunday night is a slow, relaxing evening. We never go out. We always have a quiet evening and go to bed early. It's a good way to finish the weekend before the onset of the week's activities."

What to Do with Your Time Together

Once you've planned which blocks of time will be shared, you face the decision of how much structure you prefer. If both of your personalities are such that you thrive on excitement, activities, and events, you'll undoubtedly schedule most evenings and weekends without trouble. Conversely, if you both approach life in a more laid-back, casual manner, chances are that you'll keep much of the time unstructured to do whatever your moods fancy. If you have opposing personalities, you'll need to face the issue head on.

If you have difficulty resolving this issue with your partner, consider the following questions:

1. How much structured joint time do you want? How much unstructured joint time?
2. What activities do you want to plan ahead?
3. What activities would you rather decide on at the spur of the moment?
4. What activities do you both currently have scheduled that are not flexible, e.g., college courses, evening meetings, team and league sports?

Once you answer these questions, it will be easier to get together with your partner and work out a schedule which is amenable to both of you. Table 12.1 illustrates the schedule Ella and Gary worked out.

Table 12.1

Ella and Gary's Negotiated Leisure Schedule

Weeknights: Dinner together. After dinner individual time.

Friday evening: Joint time. Go to gym or movie or party.

Saturday morning: Joint time to clean house. Lunch out together.

Saturday afternoon: Individual time.

Saturday evening: Joint time, particularly with friends.

Sunday morning: Individual time.

Sunday afternoon: Open for negotiation.

Sunday evening: Joint time at home. Television or games.

You may, however, find yourselves at loggerheads about what activities to share. What if you want to sign up for doubles tennis and your partner prefers to play bridge? Or you want to stay at home on the weekend because your job has kept you on the road all week while your partner has been home climbing the walls waiting for the weekend? What do you do if you want to celebrate your birthday at a fancy restaurant and your partner is on a strict diet?

Like any negotiation you will have to examine the many issues that surround these conflicts and make compromises or trade-offs as necessary. Can you play both bridge and tennis but on separate evenings? Or make one a weekend activity? Or alternate from week to week? Can you compromise and go out one weekend evening and stay home the other? Or if you do go out, is your partner willing to do the driving and come home early? If it's your birthday, can your partner arrange a menu selection that will be within the dietary restrictions? Or can your partner eat less the preceding and following days in order to compensate for this one meal? There may be many solutions to the various problems, you just need to discuss them fully and decide what is most appropriate.

Advanced Planning: Details that Can Make or Break an Evening

Even if you have only moderately busy schedules, you will need to do some weekly planning around your leisure time. This may be as simple as arranging for a Saturday night babysitter or phoning in dinner reservations at a favorite restaurant. Or it may become much more involved if you decide to entertain some friends at home or if you have several activities going on at the same time.

Sometimes couples fall short on these simple but necessary actions. Chuck and Shelly frequently complain that the weekend rolls around and they have nothing to do. Even if there is a movie they'd like to see, it's often too late to get a babysitter. They rarely plan activities saying that they like things to be spontaneous. Frequently they will end up bickering on the weekends because they would like to do something special but there's nothing they can do.

A few minutes of weekly planning time would solve Chuck and Shelly's problem. They need to decide what they want to do the following week and take the necessary actions to get it done. If they decide they want to play tennis on Saturday morning, go to a concert Saturday evening, and take the kids on a picnic on Sunday, they need to arrange babysitters, reserve a tennis court, purchase or reserve concert tickets, and prepare the food for the picnic. They might even want to have a backup plan if it rains on Sunday, such as going to a museum or movie.

Often the partner with the greater interest in the activity will take the initiative and work out the details, but it can be negotiated in any number of ways. Sometimes couples will alternate making the arrangements by weekends. Or they'll divide them in half. Or they'll count them as part of the household chores—weekend arrangements could equal feeding the cat, packing lunches, or paying bills.

A calendar is absolutely essential for planning leisure time activities. It should be in a prominent place, such as in the kitchen or on a bulletin board that everyone reads. As soon as plans are scheduled, they need to be posted on the calendar. It's also convenient to post names and times for babysitter pickup, food obligations, and other arrangements necessary for the event.

Also, individual activities should be posted, particularly if they're out of the ordinary. If you have a church budget meeting for Thursday evening, be sure and mention it to your partner and post it on the calendar. Then you avoid this kind of scenario: "I had hoped we could go out tonight, but you put your budget meeting ahead of me." If your partner knows about your meetings, then you can plan outings for other evenings.

A calendar is also useful in giving you a sense of how booked up you are. You can look ahead and see what weekends would be good to plan a mini-trip away. You can plan ahead important activities such as birthdays and anniversaries. When someone invites you out, you can check immediately to see if you're free.

Social Obligations

If you're not careful, obligations can ruin your life. It's important not to jeopardize your job or sever ties with your family, but you may need to learn how to say no to certain events. Cocktail parties, dinner parties, happy hours, open houses, showers, and receptions are all candidates for review. Perhaps you do need to attend certain functions. Or your partner does. But if you disagree with your partner about what is really an obligation with potential negative ramifications, then you should have a serious discussion.

You should go over the following questions when considering such events.

1. What are the consequences of my attending or not attending the event? What potential gain is there from attending? Loss from not attending?
2. Who are the key people in the power structure and what is their relationship to me?
3. Is there a way of cutting down the frequency of these obligations without totally withdrawing?
4. What options do I have for recognizing the event other than attending, e.g., send a card, flowers, make a telephone call?
5. If I choose to attend the event, how can I enjoy it more? What can I do? What can my partner do?

After reviewing these questions you may decide the risk is too great not to attend. You may stand to lose clients or you may fall out of favor at work. You might create ill will in the family. On the other hand, you may decide there are other options open to you.

After two years of visiting Dolores's family every Sunday afternoon, Ron and Dolores decided that kind of frequency was unnecessary. They decided to go every other week, explaining to the family their need for time to pursue other activities and interests. You might want to make family visits with even less frequency than this.

Similarly, your work obligations may not be as stringent as you first thought. While it may be necessary to attend the Christmas party and summer picnic, it may not be necessary to go to the bar with the office crowd every Friday after work. Nor might it be necessary to join the company softball team or bowling league. Different workplaces will have different standards and expectations of employees. If they are unclear, ask your boss and co-workers.

For those obligations that are politically necessary, think of them as work. That way you can feel a sense of accomplishment after attending an event, rather than viewing the situation as a wasted evening. Give yourself a reward for sticking it out and thank your partner if he or she also participated. Then plan another activity of your choice to compensate for this "work." Go spelunking. Make Seafood Zarzuela. Listen to "Pictures at an Exhibition."

Similarly, if you have to entertain at home, do not consider it leisure. Treat it as though it is paid employment (which it probably is, if you're developing business contacts). But also keep it fun. Most people can sense the tension if a host and hostess are on edge. Most people don't like a stuffy atmosphere but are more comfortable with informal arrangements. Take some cues from your colleagues if you're concerned about the propriety of the event you're considering. An outdoor picnic might substitute for a cocktail party, or a buffet might substitute for a formal sit-down dinner. Chapter 11 also has some suggestions for entertaining and other holiday obligations.

Parallel Play

The term "parallel play" is one used in the field of early childhood development to describe the activities of toddlers when put together in a play environment. Rather than playing together in a joint activity as older children will, these youngsters play by themselves. One child may be engrossed with a baby doll while another plays with colored blocks. The children both enjoy themselves; they are in the same room with the same toys. But they are not interacting with each other.

Adults frequently exhibit tendencies of parallel play. When Bill is watching a televised football game, he'll often ask me to join him. Since I have limited interest in football, if I decide to join him it will be doing something else such as reading or sewing. Bill has no objection and it creates a warm, friendly atmosphere. We both are pursuing our separate activities yet are present and aware of each other. I wouldn't want to spend every evening in separate activities, but on occasion it's pleasant.

Activities that lend themselves to parallel play include: puzzles, reading, listening to music, watching television, sorting recipes, needlepoint, stamp collecting, or anything that is rather low-key and relaxing. They are usually activities that are slow paced. Having someone in the room to share an occasional comment is welcome. It's a nice way to spend an occasional evening, but be warned, as a lifestyle this type of companionship can become very dull indeed. You may want to re-evaluate your situation if most of your joint time is parallel play.

If Your Partner's a Tube Boob

Are you jealous of your television set? Do you wish it had never been invented? Are you uncertain if it has been off in the past twenty-four hours? If so, your partner may very well be a tube boob.

If you do not share your partner's interest in that much television, then you're going to have to negotiate your respective priorities for leisure time.

Rule Number One: Don't initiate the discussion during your partner's favorite program. Schedule a time to negotiate this issue when neither of you is watching television. Ask your partner to bring a list of his or her "must see" favorite programs with schedules, and a second list of "want to see" programs.

Your preparation is to bring with you a list of activities you'd prefer over television watching. Indicate which ones involve your partner's participation.

As you negotiate a joint schedule be sure to build in the obvious preferences which you both have—his or her top programs and your top activities. You may be surprised that your partner is willing to join you in other activities. You may also decide to pursue your own individual interests during the time your partner is "tubing it."

If scheduling joint activities and favorite television programs is difficult, you may want to buy a VCR. VCR prices have dropped dramatically and should soon be within most people's reach. With a VCR you can tape the priority programs and play them later at a more convenient time. No machine, however, is going to instantly resolve your conflict. Only effective communication and good negotiation techniques can do this.

If Your Partner's a Fanatic

If your partner is a fanatic in any area—windsurfing, orchid gardening, or beekeeping—you will be faced with several choices.

1. *Develop your own interests and get involved in them.* While he's taking violin lessons, you can learn to sky dive.
2. *Negotiate more time together.* This will mean scheduling specific time together so your partner can still pursue his or her interests. S/he may not be aware that time is an issue for you. You may need to decide which evenings are "joint" and which ones you will use for individual interests.

3. *Join in the endeavor.* Is her enthusiasm contagious? Does he talk to you about it? Would she like you to share the interest with her?

Of course this all seems clear-cut and easily achieved. But what if your fanatic partner intrudes into your life? What if he takes over the entire basement with his art studio? What if the phone is ringing continuously with calls regarding the charity fund-raiser which she is directing? Or what if he's typing his entire recipe collection onto index cards and you need the typewriter to change your resume and type cover letters for your job search campaign?

You then have to negotiate each item specifically. Can he make do with half the basement and put the supplies in the closet when he's finished? Can you get a telephone answering machine and ask your partner to be in charge of collecting the messages? Can you ask him to use the typewriter when you're at your office so that you can have it for an hour or two every evening? Perhaps there are reasonable answers rather than to close your eyes and grit it out.

Appreciating Your Partner's Idiosyncrasies

While you may find it taxing to live with a person who raises Great Danes, weaves twenty-foot unicorn tapestries, or travels by camel through the Sahara Desert, you do have to admit that it adds some color to his or her personality. However, it may be difficult to negotiate rationally with someone who has an irrational obsession. In these cases it may be best to look at your partner with humor and recognize that the parts of the person which you love—intelligence, curiosity, dynamism, and vibrancy—all contribute to this intense interest or hobby.

Tolerance may be your defense. After all, remember her patience when you awakened her at 3:00 A.M. to look at the Southern Cross amidst a meteor shower? Or when you insisted on driving through the Everglades at midnight in order to view the phenomenon of Venus-shine? Or that she willingly spent a vacation with you in Thule, Greenland in order to observe the Aurora Borealis at its best? Everything, they say, has a price. In the long run, a little patience, tolerance, and good humor may be a small price for a partner who relishes life and pursues it with gusto.

Recommended Reading

Dorn, Sylvia O'Neill. *The How to Collect Anything Book.* Garden City, New York: Doubleday & Co., 1976.

The Great Escape: A Source Book of Delights and Pleasures for the Mind and Body. Min S. Yee, Editor, New York: Bantam Books, 1974.

The Leisure Alternatives Catalog. New York: Dell Publishing Company, 1979.

McCullagh, James C., ed. *Ways to Play.* Emmaus, Pa.: Rodale Press, Inc., 1978.

Footnotes

[1]John R. Kelly, *Leisure* (Englewood Cliffs, New Jersey: Prentice Hall, 1982), p. 9.

[2]Landon Y. Jones, *Great Expectations* (New York: Ballantine Books, 1980), p. 336.

[3]Ibid., p. 177.

13

Making It Work

Win-win negotiations may sound like a good idea for your sister and her husband or the unmarried couple next door, but is it something you can use in your own relationship? Perhaps you see yourself as different. You may be just starting out and have no discretionary income to negotiate. Or you have no conflicts about leisure activities. Or neither of you wants children. And you're both pleased with your vacation plans.

Certainly for many couples there are some issues which need not be negotiated. These are issues in which both of you view only one choice as reasonable. Fine. Leave the negotiations for those areas which provide the major (and minor) irritations in your relationship. Negotiate your desire to move to the countryside. Negotiate your desire to renovate the kitchen. Negotiate who gets the use of the one-car garage. Negotiate your brand of toothpaste. Practice with minor issues and develop the necessary skills and interplay which will prove invaluable in the future.

Also negotiate your dreams. Negotiate taking that trip to China. Or building a cabin in the woods. Or starting an antique shop. Or raising golden retrievers.

People change. Relationships change. And as you and your partner change, so will the conflicts. However, once you become skilled as a negotiator the process becomes easier. You develop a proficiency for sorting out the major issues from the details. You also become more adept at dealing with the ambiguity of complex decisions. Shall we risk having a baby with our history of medical problems? Shall we file a suit against the neighbors for property damage? Shall we insist that our grown child move out of the house unless he quits using drugs?

Not that such decisions are easy—they are often painful and agonizing—but with practice the decision-making process will become familiar. Gathering information, weighing alternate courses of action, and hearing each other's point of view can be done more thoroughly if you've had some practice on less serious issues.

At some point, however, you'll have to make your choice based on the best information and reasoning available to you. However, making the decision is only half the job; it is then up to you as a couple to make that decision work. You jointly choose your course of action—whether it is to adopt instead of having a natural child, to forget the neighbors and pay for the damage yourself, or to tell your son that he has two weeks to find a new place to live.

Then instead of worrying whether you're doing the right thing, set your course to make your action have a positive outcome. Start the adoption process. Encourage your son to get counseling. Fix the fence and lawn and add an attractive flower bed as well.

People tend to ignore the fact that they can influence the positive or negative outcome of a decision. It is here that a couple can put energy and make a decision work out well. Of course, there are many factors beyond your control and not all endings are happy, even if you do your most to make the decision work. People, through no fault of their own, may get sick, lose their jobs, and the like. In these situations mutual support and understanding is the key to survival. If you have a good relationship, you will be able to weather the crises. You will be able to endure the inevitable losses together, and you will, indeed, be winners.

Index